This item was presented by:

his family

in loving memory of
Andrew W. Poet

YJC Student Pres. 1959-60

Improving the Teaching of World Affairs

The Glens Falls Story

HAROLD M. LONG
Director of ITWA Program, Glens Falls

ROBERT N. KING
Director of Instruction, Glens Falls

NATIONAL COUNCIL FOR THE SOCIAL STUDIES
A DEPARTMENT OF THE NATIONAL EDUCATION ASSOCIATION
1201 Sixteenth Street, Northwest, Washington, D. C. 20036

Price $2.00

Foreword

NEVER has a sound, basic liberal education been more essential for each one of us than it is today. In a time of ever-increasing complexity, of ever-accelerating change, none of us can master more than a small part of the widening range of human knowledge. All the more imperative, then, is a firm understanding of essentials—the nature of the world we live in, the kind of world we are trying to build, the kind of nation we are and want to be.

Some understanding of other peoples, other cultures, other nations, is an indispensable part of a liberal education. This is true not only because our community, in essential respects, has been enlarged far beyond the county or the nation, to the point of becoming global. It is true because a knowledge of others helps us to understand ourselves—as the teachers participating in the Glens Falls Project were aware when they reported that "the more students learned about other peoples . . . the greater was their desire for a better understanding of our own nation and culture."

The project described in this report reflects great credit on the National Council for the Social Studies, the Board of Education of Glens Falls, N.Y., and all who contributed to it. It was an experimental effort in one community to broaden the mental horizons of the pupils in its classrooms, and in so doing to deepen and strengthen their understanding of the world they must live in. This is an example which should stimulate other communities and school systems to take a critical look at the preparation they are giving their young people for the responsibilities of citizenship. I hope it will be widely read.

DEAN RUSK, *Secretary of State*
United States of America

iii

Dedication

To the teachers, the students, Board of Education and the community of Glens Falls, New York, whose cooperative efforts made possible this project on "Improving the Teaching of World Affairs" the National Council for the Social Studies gratefully dedicates this report.

Preface

TEACHERS recognize the urgency and need to teach about the United States and world affairs. They know that many attitudes and opinions are formed in life and tend to be resistant to change. Because of this it is clear that our elementary and secondary schools have a vital role to play in helping to build the kind of national and world community we will have in the future. Indeed, teachers themselves must see today's world in a new perspective.

Teachers also know that the most volatile force in the world today is change—rapid change. The schools have a responsibility to educate for a changing society and to prepare students who will be able to cope with, and help direct, societal changes in the future in a manner consistent with the system of values derived from our American heritage.

While it would be naive to assume that education alone can assure a resolution of the problems confronting nations today, it would be folly to ignore the potential force and contribution that education can make in arriving at workable solutions of problems that will contribute to the goal of peace and stability in the world. This means that education must equip students with the necessary knowledge and skills that will enable them to deal with conflict and change in the future.

Students need to have a deep appreciation and understanding of their own culture as well as the cultures of other peoples. It is also important that students be made acutely aware of the harsh realities of international life and of the problems of conflicting ideologies with which we are confronted. This is essential for all people in the world— a world in which nations and people are becoming more and more interdependent, and in which they are being thrust into even closer relationships. We have reached a point in history when no nation can exist in isolation.

Because of all these facts in 1957 the National Council for the Social Studies decided to initiate a pilot action-research study on the teaching of world affairs covering all grade levels and subject matter areas. After careful thought the city Glens Falls in upstate New York (population 18,580) was invited to undertake such a study. Happily, the Board of Education and the Superintendent of Schools of Glens Falls accepted the invitation. It is even more gratifying that after the period of official sponsorship by the National Council for the Social Studies the local schools have continued the program.

We are especially indebted to the Glens Falls Board of Education, the Superintendent of Schools, the teachers in Glens Falls, and to the community itself for the splendid support and cooperation they have given to this endeavor.

We are also indebted to the individuals and groups who contributed the necessary financial support needed to make this project a reality. The sources of such support are acknowledged on page 18 of this report.

Finally, thanks are due the members of the Advisory Committee and those who served as consultants for the generous donations of time and thought they gave to the project.

Without the help of all these people the project could not have materialized.

The National Council for the Social Studies feels that it has been both a privilege and an opportunity to sponsor this project and takes pleasure in presenting this summary report on "Improving the Teaching of World Affairs" in the public schools of Glens Falls, New York. It is hoped that the work done in Glens Falls will serve as an inspiration and help to other school systems.

STELLA KERN, *President*
National Council for the Social Studies

Quotes from the Text

THE Glens Falls Project was initiated and sponsored by the National Council for the Social Studies. By this action, the National Council was responding to the revolutionary developments that in recent years have been convulsing the world and thrusting increasingly grave responsibilities upon the shoulders of educators." (*Page 15.*)

"It is expected that a more sophisticated awareness among students of the realities of international life—both hopeful and discouraging aspects, whether positive or negative—will be a result of such a program of teaching world affairs. It is important that citizens learn of the difficulties of developing a world in which nations cooperate in a responsible fashion, and of the specific obstacles and threats to peace. It is important that they learn to think clearly about solutions to world problems." (*Page 15.*)

"It is becoming increasingly clear that if education is to play the vital role envisioned for it, a new dimension of knowledge about world affairs must be made part of every school program. It is also important for us to recognize that such a program must inevitably lead to a better understanding of ourselves, and to deeper insights into the nature of our own country—its values and beliefs. It is of paramount importance that we first of all understand our own nation and have a deep commitment to the values of our society before we seek to understand other nations and their cultures." (*Page 6.*)

"This kind of program cannot be successful if it is undertaken in a pedestrian fashion. It calls for insight, dedication, and a willingness to try some new ideas, materials, and ways of teaching. This approach to teaching is a challenge which confronts education on all fronts these days. The teaching of world affairs is no exception." (*Page 9.*)

"The program for improving the teaching of world affairs," the committee declared, "is designed to have each pupil develop (1) an increasing understanding of other peoples; (2) a growing appreciation of different cultures; (3) attitudes of respect for others such as are desired for ourselves; (4) a sense of responsibility as to his personal role and the role of his country in a world of nations; and (5) an awareness of the realities of international problems." (*Page 23.*)

"These aims are to be sought through various avenues of instruction and through extracurricular activities. Every subject can contribute to the teaching of international understanding. The concern of ITWA, as its very name sets forth, is to increase the efficiency of that teaching. It is not intended that ITWA shall be identified exclusively with any one subject field. Furthermore, the ITWA program is focused as much on the elementary as on the secondary grades." *(Page 23.)*

"Not one of the persons we have just quoted—Superintendent, principal, teachers, student, community leader—spoke with publication in mind. Each had something to say, and he said it. The important consideration is that they all believed that the effort to improve the teaching of world affairs was good—good for them as individuals, good for the schools and the community, good for the country, and good for the world." (*Page 72.*)

Table of Contents

CHAPTER ONE

The Glens Falls Story

MERRILL F. HARTSHORN
Executive Secretary, NCSS

"Civilization, it was once said, is a race between
education and catastrophe—and we intend to win
the race for education."—*John F. Kennedy*

Man has only begun to reach
for a stable world order through the education of youth. What
could happen if we really made an all-out effort to achieve such
a goal?

It occurred to a small group of educators thinking about this
problem that one of the failures of today's violent world was a
partial failure of education. They wondered what would happen
if a deliberate effort were made in education, starting with the
kindergarten, to educate people to understand one another better. If such a program proved successful, and if it were tried in
many communities, perhaps the path to eventual world peace
would be made smoother.

Can education, religion, and science pool their resources in an
intensive effort aimed at building a stable world order? Can
education reduce, or eliminate, stereotypes, distrust, and fear of
responsible cooperation, which has led, and is threatening to lead
the world into a series of destructive disasters? Can education
aid in improving communication and understanding among people and nations?

We believe the answer is "Yes." At the very least educators must
believe that progress can be made in this direction or we can have
no hope for the future.

To help provide some knowledge on how to direct education

1

towards the goals suggested a pioneer program was launched six years ago in the public school system of Glens Falls, New York.

PURPOSE OF THE PROJECT

The importance of providing sound instruction in elementary and secondary schools about other peoples and their cultures and about this country's role in world affairs is obvious. Pupils must acquire an understanding about the complexities of the world in which they live. They should practice methods of inquiry and become expert in the use of various sources of information. The ability of citizens, young and old, to think clearly and constructively about the role of the United States in world affairs is prerequisite to the development and implementation of wise national policies. This is vital to our own national interest and perhaps also to the survival of mankind.

American citizens must become sensitive to other cultures, conscious of the complexities of intercultural relations, humane in their outlook. They must feel a deep sense of personal obligation for the general welfare. Schools should use all available resources in an effort to achieve these outcomes. This country's future, indeed its very existence, may well depend on our success or failure in helping pupils learn the dimensions of world problems and what this country can and should do about them.

For many years our schools have been making a sincere effort to teach about world affairs. Much has been written and spoken on this subject, and especially about goals and ways of achieving them. Unfortunately no school system, having formulated goals to be sought through instruction, had made an *intensive* effort at *all* grade levels and in *every* subject in the curriculum to provide a cumulative record of the results of teaching world affairs until the Glens Falls Project. Thus we have known comparatively little about how effective our teaching of world affairs has been. Too much of the writing on this subject has been hortatory.

Some educational efforts in this area have been bitterly attacked by pressure groups. In some communities programs have had to be abandoned because citizens generally had little knowledge of what the schools were trying to do and why. Community support and understanding must be an integral part of any realistic program designed to further an understanding of world affairs in our schools.

The reasons given above will suggest why the National Council for the Social Studies initiated a pilot action-research project in Glens Falls in 1957 that was given the name "Improving the Teaching of World Affairs," or "ITWA."

NATURE OF THE PROJECT

This project called for a full-scale effort in one selected school system to improve education about world affairs. This was to be done through the involvement of teachers in every aspect of the school program at both the elementary and secondary school levels. The first step, naturally, was to identify an appropriate school system—a small city system in which there existed good educational leadership and happy school-community relations—a system able and willing to cooperate in a three-year program to improve the teaching of world affairs. While the policy direction of the study was to be entrusted to a special NCSS committee, and funds for its partial support administered by the Council, the full and hearty cooperation of the selected school system was essential. Local school authorities were always in control and no steps were taken without their full approval. In reality the project was developed and carried out by Glens Falls school personnel.

Having selected a school system, arrangements were completed by which an outstanding social studies teacher in that system was made Project Director. It was considered desirable that the Director be well known in the school system and have the support and confidence of the school administration, teachers, and the citizens of the community. He was released from most of his teaching in order to give major attention to the project. In cooperation with teachers, supervisors, administrators, and the sponsoring NCSS committee he was given the responsibility to: (a) evaluate the understanding of world affairs possessed by students at various grade levels, (b) assume responsibility for securing (and give direction to the preparation of) materials needed for instruction and evaluation, (c) develop, with the assistance of teachers and consultants, ways in which the teaching of world affairs could be incorporated into the school curriculum at each grade level in all subject matter areas, and in extracurricular activities, and (d) make continuing formal and informal efforts to appraise the results. The techniques and materials utilized were designed so that once their value had been established they could be adapted for use in other school systems. This last point is important since it insures that other school systems could profit from the experience of the pilot school system.

The project continued over a three-year period, and was developed in a coordinated fashion, systematically improved through experimentation, continuously evaluated in a variety of ways. Thus the project could prove to be the first major action-research program designed to explore the ways and means whereby a school can improve instruction about world affairs. The project should be of direct and enduring value to the school system concerned, and it is hoped that this report will stimulate and prove helpful to other schools and teacher training institutions seeking to improve the teaching of world affairs.

The program developed within the Glens Falls school system involved all appropriate subjects, teachers, and school services. The Director secured the cooperation of many outside agencies offering consultation, materials, or services related to the subject of the experiment. This description of the Glens Falls program provides useful insight into how to identify and make use of the available resources in a project of this kind.

One outcome of the Glens Falls Project was the production of such teaching aids and units as the following: other peoples and other lands—their history, institutions, value systems, and ways of life; United States foreign policy and the forces which helped shape it; causes of war; international organizations and the machinery for peace; the United States as a democratic nation in a world setting; conflicting ideologies in today's world. Among other approaches were activities focused on: the comparative study of student art from schools in several countries; comparative business methods, merchandising and office practices in other countries; foods and families of the world; health and disease problems of the world; the literature and culture of other countries in English and foreign language classes; mathematics as a means of international communication; music of Western and non-Western cultures; physical education, games, and recreation in other lands; and the technology of business and industry in other nations. Bibliographies that include both audio-visual and printed materials were prepared for the use of teachers. A service was established to coordinate the use of classroom periodicals, radio, television, news magazines and newspapers in the several schools.

Foreign visitors and government officials were used as resource persons. So were special consultants on curriculum and evaluation, and persons who were experts on topics of special interest to teachers. Such activities as pen pal correspondence, stamp collections, schoolwide assembly programs, speaking before community groups, making arrangements for foreign guests, planning model assemblies of the United Nations, and others were used to further the goal of improving the understanding of world affairs throughout the total school program.

The production of tests and means of evaluating the outcomes of the program was a vital part of the project. There is a great need to discover what techniques and materials are effective in teaching about world affairs. In this facet of the project specialists in evaluation played significant roles.

It is expected that a more sophisticated awareness among students of the realities of international life—both hopeful and discouraging aspects, whether positive or negative—will be a result of such a program of teaching world affairs. It is important that citizens learn of the difficulties of developing a world in which nations cooperate in a responsible fashion, and of the specific obstacles and threats to peace. It is important that they learn to think clearly about solutions to world problems. This is precisely why such a program designed to improve the teaching of world affairs is so necessary. Without such education in our schools we run the grave risk of naive, volatile and immature public response to the dangerous challenges that confront us.

Today, as we pay increasing attention to the world outside the United States, we are confronted with problems of conflicting ideologies. Education has become identified as a vital part of our national defense and our national goals. For example, with the gains that Russia has made in the space age we find that schools are being urged to develop improved programs in science and mathematics to keep us ahead of Russian gains. The schools also are being asked to teach about communism as part of our total defense effort.

It is becoming increasingly clear that if education is to play the vital role envisioned for it, a new dimension of knowledge about world affairs must be made part of every school program. It is also important for us to recognize that such a program must inevitably lead to a better understanding of ourselves, and to deeper insights into the nature of our own country—its values and beliefs. It is of paramount importance that we first of all understand our own nation and have a deep commitment to the values of our society before we seek to understand other nations and their cultures.

OVERVIEW OF OUTCOMES

Having learned why the Glens Falls Project was undertaken and the basic goals it was designed to further, the reader will naturally wonder, "What were the outcomes?" This over-all question is answered at length in Chapters 3 to 7. To provide an overview of the entire report, we shall list and answer briefly a few questions most often asked by teachers, administrators, and laymen who have written or visited Glens Falls to learn more about the experiment.

1. *What role did the Board of Education and the school administration play in the program?*

The Board of Education formally approved the guiding principles developed for the project and also its budget. After the completion of the three years of the experiment, the Board absorbed some of the costs earlier met from outside sources and continued arrangements to insure that the emphasis on the teaching of world affairs would continue. Individual members of the Board in a great variety of ways demonstrated their interest in ITWA.

The Superintendent formally gave his approval to the project and gave invaluable advice for its implementation. He named the Director of ITWA to the Curriculum Council, and the Director later became chairman of a subcommittee which included teachers from several subject fields at various grade levels. The Curriculum Council has the Superintendent as chairman and includes all principals and at least one teacher from each school and deals with all curricular problems that require attention.

2. *Were teachers of various subjects at various grade levels receptive to suggestions that more of the teaching and classroom time be devoted to teaching an understanding of world affairs?*

In many cases it was not a matter of giving more time but of using time differently. In general teachers appreciated suggestions with respect to materials and methods, and the scheduling of films and resource persons, including visitors from overseas. Members of the faculty who were not teaching social studies were enthusiastic about showing contributions which could be made by their subject fields. Teachers willingly gave their time to conferences and workshops.

In general, it was easier for elementary than for high school teachers to make adjustments in teaching programs. And, of course, there were differences among teachers at any grade level. The fact remains that teachers from all grade levels and all subject fields contributed to the success of the program.

3. *What was the attitude of the community toward the program?*

There was a high degree of community support, involving a variety of organizations and agencies, and a great number of individuals.

The support of the press, churches, luncheon and patriotic groups is noteworthy. So, also, is the way in which families opened their homes to foreign visitors who came to Glens Falls.

Community support manifested itself not only in attendance at related school and community functions, but also through financial contributions to help support ITWA activities.

4. *Did this program call for a large expenditure of funds?*

About $15,000 per year in outside funds were made available for three years to support ITWA. But it does not follow that a school system cannot improve the teaching of world affairs unless it receives this amount of outside support. In a typical situation, changes may be made more gradually. Quite possibly many of the items for which funds are needed will already be included in the school budget. Among such items are: books, periodicals, films, supplies; travel funds for teachers and funds to bring consultants to the community; budgeted time and funds for curriculum and evaluation committees; budgeted time and funds for the in-service education of teachers—workshops, conferences, school visitation, travel.

5. *What was the effect of the program on the general scholastic achievement in all subject matter areas?*

Doubtless the thought of being involved in an experiment and doing something new and different inspires students and teachers to greater effort.

Students in all subject fields did well in terms of performance on conventional achievement tests. There was no suggestion that ITWA interfered with "regular teaching." Indeed ITWA was enthusiastically accepted as an essential ingredient in, and enrichment of, the total school program.

6. *Could this type of program be carried out readily in other communities?*

The answer is "Yes." It should be noted, however, that ITWA involved cooperation between school and community, faculty and administration, the local system and nearby educational institutions and agencies. ITWA's success also depended on the "know-how" demonstrated by the Director and members of the school administration in identifying and using a variety of resources. It should be added that Glens Falls had been resourceful along these lines before ITWA was established.

7. *What were some of the significant experiences that resulted in improving instruction?*

The visits of teachers and students from overseas—often at no cost to the school—helped immeasurably in introducing new points of view and in motivating students to learn about other cultures. At the same time the teachers discovered that the more students learned about other peoples, cultures, and nations the greater was their desire for a better understanding of our own nation and culture. So far as the teachers were concerned the opportunities for in-service education about world affairs, and for information about geographic regions concerning which they knew little were greatly appreciated. The special conferences and workshops were a means of making teachers better informed and, therefore, more secure in their pioneering efforts. Once the teachers had the information at hand they showed great ingenuity and creativity in teaching procedures.

CONCLUDING OBSERVATIONS

The answers to these questions provide a kind of overview of the project as it was carried out. However, these brief remarks cannot do the project justice; the reader should read this report in its entirety. The chapters that follow contain information regarding the setting for the project and some of the activities carried out in the schools. They contain also judgments about outcomes. In each chapter an effort has been made to include the essential facts.

The reader of this report, however, can readily fail to identify and take into account one vital component. That is the enthusiasm and zeal of the teachers and students for the project—without this and the leadership of the Superintendent of Schools the project would have been less successful. This kind of program cannot be successful if it is undertaken in a pedestrian fashion. It calls for insight, dedication, and a willingness to try some new ideas, materials, and ways of teaching. This approach to teaching is a challenge which confronts education on all fronts these days. The teaching of world affairs is no exception.

CHAPTER TWO

Glens Falls

URING the winter of 1959-1960, a British reporter visited Albany to interview Governor Nelson A. Rockefeller, then a prominent contender for the Republican Presidential nomination. In his dispatch to England, the reporter, after lingering at some length on the colorful background of New York's capital, observed with tongue in cheek that north of Albany there was little more than two thousand miles of ice and snow.

Among the upstate New Yorkers who read this intriguing but decidedly misleading observation with wry amusement were the citizens of Glens Falls, a community of some 18,000 people (according to the 1960 census) located about 50 miles north of the state capital. In the first place, as every knowledgeable inhabitant of the city knows, Glens Falls has never been isolated from the larger world beyond its boundaries. On the contrary, and more perhaps than many towns, the history of the community, which dates back to well before the American Revolution, has always included, and still does include, direct and immediate ties to the national and international scene. In the second place, since 1957 the city has been the center for the pilot program in international education which is the subject of this report. During the six years from 1957 through 1963, the program known as "Improving the Teaching of World Affairs," or ITWA for short, attracted more than 200 visitors from 60 different countries to the community, and was largely responsible for motivating many Glens Falls citizens, among them public school students, to travel and study abroad. Land of ice and snow, indeed! But the flow of people from many lands in and out of a relatively small American city is only a dramatic by-product of the developments set in motion by the ITWA Project. Before we turn to the Glens Falls Project, however, a brief look at the community, past and present, may be helpful.

It is interesting to note, although the fact may be important only as a symbol, that Glens Falls has always been a "gateway community." When it was founded in 1763 by Abraham Wing, who later built a sawmill at the falls over which the Hudson River plunges on its way to the sea, the settlement and the region immediately surrounding it stood astride "the Great Northern Gateway" between Canada and the British colonies along the Atlantic seaboard. Earlier, before the first Europeans arrived in the New World, Indian war parties traveled the Hudson River-Lake George-Lake Champlain route north and south through the wilderness. During the century-long struggle between France and England for control of North America, armies of French and British troops, together with their colonial contingents and their Indian allies, surged back and forth across this then strategically valuable region. And in 1777, the settlement of Wing's Falls, which eleven years later was renamed by Colonel John Glen, Glen's Falls, stood near the center of the area in which American troops defeated General Burgoyne's army in the decisive Battle of Saratoga and halted the British thrust southward from Canada.

Today Glens Falls (the apostrophe was dropped many years ago) is called "the Gateway to the Adirondacks." The Indian trails are gone, and the military roads that ran north and south during the French and Indian War and the American Revolution have been replaced by modern highways over which tourists, by the countless thousands, travel north to summer cottages and resort comunities scattered along the shores of the lakes and through the mountains. Route 9 and Route 87, major north and south highways, cross the Hudson River by bridges at Glens Falls and the city has become a market and supply center for the hotels and other resort establishments around Lake George and in the southern Adirondack Mountains.

For more than a hundred years, before modern highways replaced dirt roads and opened up the region as a resort area, the economic backbone of Glens Falls was lumbering and quarrying—

limestone along the river banks, and a choice variety of black marble. By the end of the nineteenth century, however, the forests which had once provided what seemed at the time to be an inexhaustible supply of timber were rapidly vanishing. One by one the sawmills ended their operations. Deprived of the fuel upon which it depended, the lime industry also began to decline.

During the past fifty years the older extractive industries have been largely replaced by commerce and diversified manufacturing, including paper, wallpaper, chemicals, pigment colors, shirts, collars, fabric gloves, dresses, textiles, and machines. Cement and insurance also figure prominently in the economic life of the community. Many of the industries are locally owned. Of these, the majority of the chief officers and major stockholders live in Glens Falls or the immediate vicinity. Dividends, the salaries of the managerial group, and the wages of the skilled workers remain for the most part in the city. As a result Glens Falls is a relatively prosperous community in which most of the people own their homes and earn their living in the local industries.

Through the years Glens Falls has been an unusually stable community. A substantial number of the citizens are descended from families that settled in the town during the early years of its history. Many more families represent the second and third generations to live in the community. Unlike most industrial areas, Glens Falls has never had to absorb a sudden influx of newcomers. Indeed, between 1908 and 1950 the population increased by only 4,000, from 15,000 to 19,000 and then shrank to the present 18,000. Suburban growth, meanwhile, has been more rapid. The quiet tree-lined streets, with the houses surrounded by green lawns, bear silent witness to the orderly growth of the town. More eloquent testimony to the character of the community appeared a number of years ago when, during World War II, *Look* magazine called Glens Falls "Home Town—U. S. A." and described it as "the community most soldiers want to come back to."

Would the project we are about to describe operate as successfully in a less stable, less homogeneous community? This question, raised repeatedly by observers who visited Glens Falls to learn at first hand what the program in international education was all about, cannot be answered until further undertakings of a similar nature are conducted elsewhere. The most that can be said is that Glens Falls seemed to offer a favorable climate for a project requiring the wholehearted cooperation of the schools, the businesses, the service and civic organizations, and the citizens in general.

Glens Falls did, however, enjoy one advantage which on the record contributed materially to the success of the program. A number of industries, several of them relatively small and locally owned, are interested in the international market. Merely by way of illustration, for the examples could be multiplied endlessly, one of the branch offices of the Glens Falls Insurance Company recently bonded the delivery of a dry dock that had to be moved by water from the Philippines to Kuwait at the head of the Persian Gulf; the Imperial Department of the Hercules Powder Company receives large periodic shipments of chromite ore from Lourenco Marques, Mozambique, on the east coast of Africa; the General Electric Plant at Hudson Falls, three miles from Glens Falls but considered part of the Glens Falls community, does a substantial amount of business with Latin America; and the Sandy Hill Iron and Brass Works, also of Hudson Falls, which has manufactured and installed papermaking machinery in many papermaking states in the United States and in many countries around the world, recently completed the installation of a paper mill for the Government Printing Agency on the outskirts of Taejon in Korea. Using rags and other salvageable material, the Korean mill produces paper for cigarettes and currency. Incidentally, the bond for the delivery and installation of the machinery was provided by the Glens Falls Insurance Company.

There is, of course, nothing unique in the fact that business, large or small, is interested in international trade. Every industrial area, particularly where diversified manufacturing predominates, could match the Glens Falls examples without the slightest difficulty. But there is an additional aspect in the Glens Falls situation which, although again not unique, is certainly not universal. This is the genuine and demonstrable interest of many Glens Falls businessmen in the human side of the equation. We are referring to an attitude, to a point of view about people. For example, when the Korean paper mill was being constructed several of the principal officers of the Sandy Hill Iron and Brass Works went to Korea to supervise personally the installation of the machinery. About a year and a half later the President of the Sandy Hill company happened to hear, quite incidentally, that a group of twenty-two bankers from Korea were on tour in the United States. He located them in Boston and with a few properly placed telephone calls was able to interrupt the tour, and, with the cooperation of friends, drive to Boston and escort the twenty-two bankers to Glens Falls. There he entertained them at a dinner to which he had invited bankers from Glens Falls and from other communities as far away as Albany.

The Glens Falls community, including the citizenry in general as well as businessmen, is genuinely interested in establishing communication with people from other lands. How much of this interest can be attributed to the influence of the project, "Improving the Teaching of World Affairs," it is impossible to say. There is, however, abundant evidence that interest and enthusiasm began to rise perceptibly after the program was started in the fall of 1957. In the early months, for instance, the Director of the project more often than not personally invited families to house and to help entertain overseas visitors and exchange students. Today, the Director's file contains a growing list of names of families who wish to serve as hosts for "the next visitors." The doors are open, and each of the seven Congolese teachers who spent several days in Glens Falls in 1961 could, if he had been asked, have had his choice of several hosts. Incidentally, but worth careful note, Glens Falls was one of the few places on their tour in which the visitors from the Congo had an opportunity to live in American homes and to get a firsthand glimpse of family life.

But we are now ahead of our story. If it had not been for the Glens Falls Project, the chances are that most of the foreign travelers, including the Congolese, would have remained unaware of even the name of the small city on the upper reaches of the Hudson River.

CHAPTER THREE

The Beginning

THE Glens Falls Project was initiated and sponsored by the National Council for the Social Studies. By this action, the National Council was responding to the revolutionary developments that in recent years have been convulsing the world and thrusting increasingly grave responsibilities upon the shoulders of educators.

There is no need in this report to dwell at length upon the developments that in our time have been transforming life everywhere on earth. A word or two about the nature of the changes confronting us is, however, in order, for the full significance of the venture in international education carried on in Glens Falls can be appreciated only when it is placed in this larger perspective.

Ours is a shrinking world. Measured in terms of communications and transportation, the globe on which we live has been growing smaller and smaller with disconcerting speed.

Ours is also a widening world. Measured in terms of the new situations men face, the world has been expanding at a startling rate. During the past two or three decades mankind has been faced with an unprecedented and ever-accelerating accumulation of knowledge, a phenomenal growth of population, the emergence of new nations, the world-wide revolution of rising expectations, the staggering complexity of economic and social and political problems, and the increasing interdependence of men and nations.

As a consequence of these developments, the local community is now local only in the sense that it occupies a small and measurable area of the globe. The problems of the world have burst

15

into every home, and the individual who gives a thought for the morrow finds himself looking out toward intellectual horizons that are literally limitless and into a future that defies even the most fertile imagination. Add the Cold War and the haunting threat of a nuclear holocaust to the problems men face, then the case for readjustments in outlook, institutions, and established practices becomes compelling.

"No man is an Island, intire of itselfe," John Donne wrote in an earlier and simpler age. By the 1950's this truth had assumed the dimensions of a warning that mankind could no longer afford to ignore. It was obvious to all who gave the matter any thought that an education which had served well enough, even a decade or two ago, was no longer adequate for a generation that was being hurled into an uncertain future with breathtaking speed.

But what kind of education *will* prepare this generation to live today and tomorrow as creative individuals and as intellectually competent, morally responsible citizens? It is hardly necessary to argue that the answer men give to this question, not only in the United States but in every country in the world, must exercise a decisive influence upon the future of civilization itself.

During the years since World War II, social studies teachers working as individuals and through their professional associations, including the National Council for the Social Studies, have revealed their awareness of the urgent need to develop a vital program of social education. At no time in the history of American education has there been such a widespread and earnest effort involving re-evaluation, experimentation, and revision. Many of the proposals have created vigorous, even heated, controversy. But there has been widespread acceptance of the proposition that education in general and the social studies in particular must be reoriented to provide a world point of view.

Such, in brief, was the climate of thinking that prompted the National Council to begin to explore the possibility of conducting in a single school system a pilot study aimed at discovering the most effective ways to arouse in students a greater awareness of and knowledge about world affairs. During the course of a series of preliminary conferences, William L. Breese, a public-spirited citizen with a deep personal commitment to the improvement of international relations, and a friend of the National Council, indicated his willingness to underwrite a share of the cost of a three-year pilot study-action program. Encouraged by this offer of financial support, the members of the National Council committee,[1] after tentatively selecting Glens Falls as a suitable location for the undertaking, invited Harold M. Long, head of the social studies department in the Junior-Senior High School of the city, to meet with them and with Mr. Breese to discuss the feasibility of the proposal.

Why Glens Falls? We have already given a partial answer to this question.

In general, as we reported earlier, the community as a whole had a record of genuine interest in the development of international understanding. The local lecture platform had served as a forum for public discussion of national and international issues. Exchange teachers had taught in the schools, and a significant number of faculty members had traveled in other lands. For several years civic and fraternal groups had sponsored and financed a "Community Ambassador" program through which each summer two young people were given the opportunity to travel overseas.

Aside from these general considerations, the Glens Falls school system offered certain advantages for the proposed pilot program. Over a period of years it had received consistently high ratings from competent educational surveys for the quality of its instruction. Equally important, the Superintendent and his administrative assistants had demonstrated both vision and capacity for leadership. Many members of the staff had been active in state and national professional organizations, including the National Council for the Social Studies.

But would Glens Falls agree to conduct the proposed attempt to improve instruction? And would the directors of the National Council accept the recommendation of its committee? Before either of these questions could be answered, the committee had to draft a firm proposal outlining the nature of the project. The

---

[1] The committee consisted of NCSS Executive Secretary Merrill F. Hartshorn; President-Elect William H. Cartwright; and Howard E. Wilson, Dean of the School of Education at UCLA and formerly Assistant Director, Division of Education of the Carnegie Endowment for International Peace.

proposal included a concise list of five guiding principles and an estimated budget. When this proposal was presented to the Board of Education of the Glens Falls City School District and the Board of Directors of the National Council, both organizations immediately gave their approval. The time had come to launch the project, "Improving the Teaching of World Affairs."

At this point, however, it is important to pause for a careful look at the guiding principles and the proposed budget. Considered together, the principles and the amount of money required to finance the pilot study take us directly to the very heart of the project.

There is a deceptive simplicity in the following statement of guiding principles: *First,* the effort to develop a heightened awareness of and increased sensitivity to the larger world should be a matter of primary concern to the entire school system, including teachers at every grade level and of every subject. *Second,* the project should be established *within* the framework of the existing curriculum. *Third,* the full resources of the school should be utilized in the process of teaching and evaluation, including the work carried on in the area of so-called extracurricular activities. *Fourth,* the local community should be involved as directly and as completely as possible. *Fifth,* the budget should be held to a minimum in order to demonstrate that a similar program could be conducted in any other community willing to make the necessary effort.

The budget provided $15,000 for each of the three years. These funds, secured by the sponsoring organization in the form of grants,[2] enabled the school system to employ an additional

---

[2] In addition to the contribution made by William L. Breese, grants-in-aid were made by the National Education Association, the Helen Dwight Reid Educational Foundation, *Time* magazine, *The New York Times,* and an anonymous donor. At the beginning of the third year when funds were not on hand to complete the program, the Glens Falls community stepped in with financial support. Hubert C. Brown made a personal contribution, and the Glens Falls Foundation, a local philanthropy, gave a grant of $2,000. In the spring of 1960 the Carnegie Endowment for International Peace also contributed financial support. Additional assistance came in the form of books and other instructional materials from publishers and various agencies and organizations. The Japan Society contributed books and leaflets; the Asia Society, teaching materials and a cash grant for books in connection with a course for teachers; the Denoyer-Geppert Company, 200 map calendars for classroom use. Civic Education Service and Scholastic Magazines also generously contributed teaching aids.

teacher. This in turn made it possible to release the head of the social studies department from a part of his classroom assignments to serve as Director of the project. It also enabled the Director to employ an office secretary, to engage the services of consultants on subject matter, on curriculum and on evaluation, and provided funds to cover the expenses of meetings of an Advisory Committee.

Before proceeding to an examination of the on-going program in Glens Falls, including the matter of evaluation and the role of the Advisory Committee, we turn to a significant conclusion that needs to be drawn from the statement of principles. The Glens Falls Project was essentially an effort to reorient the thinking and the attitudes of everyone involved. Although the social studies had a central role to play, a fully successful outcome depended upon the degree to which the effort could mobilize the complete resources of the educational system *and* the community.

This point, which sounds so obvious when it is simply stated, continued to elude many observers during the course of the project, as many inquiries show. For example, one letter came from an educator who had heard about the ITWA program and was seeking further information. "We are about to revise our curriculum," the writer began, "and we would like to use the material you have prepared in our social studies improvement work. Will you please place our name on your mailing list for the report of your study."

This letter, typical of a large number accumulated by the Director, reveals a basic if understandable misconception in regard to both the purpose and the nature of the experiment. The writer of the letter, together with those who share his expectations, will look in vain in this report for a neatly patterned social studies program that can be lifted in its entirety and adopted by other schools.

At no time during the course of ITWA, either in the early stages or when it was in full swing, did any of the leading participants think primarily in terms of new courses of study or a new curriculum. This is not to say that the participants, or the Director of the project, were indifferent to the development of new units of work, the revision of existing courses, or the reorganization of the curriculum. Quite the contrary was true. But the major purpose of the project was to stimulate the teachers, and through them the students and the citizens in the local community, to enlarge their perspective of the world around them. The Director assumed that an increased sensitivity to world affairs, a realistic world outlook, if you will, would lead in time to far-reaching changes in the entire curriculum. But the reorientation had to come first. Otherwise, efforts at revising the curriculum, no matter how carefully carried on, would provide at worst a patchwork operation and at best a program that lacked a sense of direction and a unifying purpose.

Seeking to reveal the essential nature of the project, the ITWA Director frequently began his explanation with a quotation from Kipling:

"Winds of the World, give answer! They
    are whimpering to and fro—
And what should they know of England
    who only England know?"[3]

In what is probably a somewhat more familiar quotation, Robert Burns also emphasized the necessity for enlarging our perspectives:

"Oh wad some power the giftie
    gie us
To see oursels as others see us!"[4]

These two quotations provide the clearest possible insight into the fundamental purpose of the project, "Improving the Teaching of World Affairs." With this understanding and the desire to reorient its thinking, it would be a simple matter for any school system in any community across the face of the earth to move, as Glens Falls did, toward a solution to one of the most urgent problems facing mankind in our time: namely, the need to understand and appreciate the common humanity of all men everywhere. Given the nature of the world in which we are now living, there can be no future for any of us without this understanding and this appreciation.

---

[3] From "The English Flag" by Rudyard Kipling.
[4] From "To a Louse" by Robert Burns.

CHAPTER FOUR

Organizing for Action

T HE ITWA staff consisted of a Director, two part-time associated teachers, and an office secretary. It operated out of an office in the high school. "Operated out of" is the correct description, for this was an action program.

It is also important to note that the ITWA staff was not superimposed upon the educational system. On the contrary, it was incorporated into the existing machinery where, from the outset, it functioned as an integral part of the entire educational program. Since much of the success of the project can be attributed to efficient organization, a brief outline of the organizational and administrative arrangements within which the project functioned should be instructive.

For several years before ITWA was launched, all curricular matters in the Glens Falls Schools were under constant review by a Curriculum Council. The Council, organized by former Superintendent A. W. Miller, has been continued by Superintendent Douglass B. Roberts. With the Superintendent as chairman, the Council consisted of approximately 25 members, including a representative of the Board of Education, the principals of the seven schools, at least one classroom teacher from each school, and additional teachers to insure that the points of view of all instructional areas were represented. The Council met about once each month. At these meetings it discussed curricular problems requiring attention and areas of the curriculum calling for study and evaluation. As a normal procedure, the Council appointed subcommittees, on each of which a member of the Council usually served as chairman, to study the specific problems and to draft recommendations for action. In the past the Council had followed this procedure in its evaluation of permanent record cards, testing programs for all grades from kindergarten through twelve, the reading program, the teaching of English, and an Honors Program for the Senior High School.

In the autumn of 1957, the new World Affairs Project became an integral part of this machinery. The Superintendent named the ITWA Director to the Curriculum Council. The latter became chairman of a subcommittee for ITWA. Membership on the subcommittee reflected every grade level and subject taught in the school system. As the project developed the subcommittee planned workshops for teachers, studied teaching methods and materials, kept in close touch with every aspect of the program, and reported regularly to the Curriculum Council.

In addition to his membership on the Curriculum Council and his chairmanship of the subcommittee on ITWA, the Project Director in the official capacity of supervisor had direct access to every classroom. By these organizational arrangements the World Affairs Project was tied into the long-term and over-all curriculum planning for the school system as a whole as well as into the day-by-day classroom activities.

An Advisory Committee formed another essential branch of the ITWA organization. Appointed by the Board of Directors of the National Council for the Social Studies, the seven members of this committee were instructed to serve as trustees of the ITWA funds and to meet periodically in Glens Falls for consultation with the Superintendent of Schools and the ITWA Director.[5] These meetings usually lasted for two or three days.

The Advisory Committee held its first meeting in October, 1957. At this meeting the committee compiled a list of consultants, among them subject-matter specialists, who might be useful as the program developed; proposed a plan for evaluating the project; and drafted a guiding statement of philosophy and

---

[5] The members of the Advisory Committee were Howard R. Anderson, University of Rochester (chairman); William H. Cartwright, Duke University; Delia Goetz, International Cooperation Administration; Merrill F. Hartshorn, Executive Secretary of the National Council for the Social Studies; Preston E. James, Syracuse University; Allen Y. King, Cleveland (Ohio) Public Schools; and Robert J. Solomon, Educational Testing Service, Princeton, New Jersey.

practice. This statement, which bore the title "An Orientation to Tasks Involved in Improving the Teaching of World Affairs," was mimeographed and made available to the teachers. It served as a highly useful directive to all members of the staff. Each of the five divisions of the orientation paper embodied both suggestions and recommendations.

ORIENTATION TO TASKS

In *Part I* the committee clarified the objectives of the ITWA Project.

"The program for improving the teaching of world affairs," the committee declared, "is designed to have each pupil develop (1) an increasing understanding of other peoples; (2) a growing appreciation of different cultures; (3) attitudes of respect for others such as are desired for ourselves; (4) a sense of responsibility as to his personal role and the role of his country in a world of nations; and (5) an awareness of the realities of international problems.

"These aims are to be sought through various avenues of instruction and through extracurricular activities. Every subject can contribute to the teaching of international understanding. The concern of ITWA, as its very name sets forth, is to increase the efficiency of that teaching. It is not intended that ITWA shall be identified exclusively with any one subject field. Furthermore, the ITWA program is focused as much on the elementary as on the secondary grades.

"The goal of education for international understanding is a world in which all peoples (1) know as much as possible about other peoples and why they live as they do; (2) keep informed about problems and issues tending to divide peoples; (3) use their influence to settle those issues in accordance with universal values and through appeals to reason rather than emotion; (4) are sincerely interested in helping other peoples to live the good life and are willing to make sacrifices to that end; (5) realistically appraise national goals and the extent to which these can be modified to conciliate other peoples, as well as the point at which yielding in the face of pressure achieves no lasting good; and (6) consider carefully those responsibilities that under present conditions can reasonably be assigned to agencies for international cooperation, and those which must be provided for in some other way.

"In education for international understanding we should try to promote a comprehension of the ways of life, the values, and the aspirations of all peoples of the world. And we should try to achieve an understanding of the requirements of living together on this planet. In this sense 'understanding' includes the necessity of comprehending our own ways of living, as well as the ways of other peoples. In short, international understanding should lead to the ability to observe and appraise, critically and objectively, the conduct of men everywhere toward each other, irrespective of the nationality or culture to which they may belong. . . ."

Part II of the orientation paper began by emphasizing the revolutionary character of the age in which we are living. It then went on to urge those involved in the ITWA program to question, soberly and critically and with a deep sense of responsibility, whether the existing educational program did in fact provide an adequate education for young people growing up in this "unique period in human history." Perhaps, the committee suggested, a social studies program that devoted greater attention to the cultural areas of the world, as distinct from the more traditional study of nations, would provide fresh insights into the nature of the social realities and, by making use of the findings of sociologists, anthropologists, and other behavioral and social scientists, reveal possibilities for adding depth and meaning to the curriculum. The committee made it clear, however, that it was not recommending a drastic reorganization of the social studies program. That was not its business. When it singled out the cultural area concept for special consideration, it was merely suggesting one of a number of ways by which teachers could stand back and re-evaluate their work from a fresh perspective.

In *Part III* of the orientation paper, the committee stressed the importance of the systematic development of intellectual skills "at all grade levels and in all areas of the school program." The development of the skill to think critically, and to be able to analyze crucial issues, was a constant objective of the program.

In *Part IV*, it turned to the problem of evaluating the outcome of the ITWA experiment and offered a number of specific recommendations. We shall deal with these recommendations and the evaluation process itself in a later section of this report.

Part V of the orientation paper contained a list of concrete suggestions for getting the project underway with a minimum of waste motion. Specifically, the committee recommended that the faculty:

1. Catalog those ideas and practices contributing to an understanding of world relationships which had already proven successful in Glens Falls.
2. Begin at once to develop new ideas and activities to add to the list.
3. Establish a workable method for sharing these "promising practices" among all the teachers in the several schools.
4. Prepare a list of the human and material resources in Glens Falls (and elsewhere) that could be utilized in the program.
5. Examine each subject to determine the extent to which it could be used to further international understanding *without* diverting it from its original purpose.
6. Examine each subject with the idea of determining the extent to which it could contribute materials or ideas useful for the teaching of international understanding in other subject areas.
7. Undertake both as individuals, and in a systematic way as a group, to develop through reading and discussion a sharper awareness of and knowledge about the contemporary world, and explore ways in which this increased understanding could be turned to account in the classroom.

The Advisory Committee presented its suggestions and recommendations to the faculty at a special meeting held (of all times!) on a Saturday afternoon. The fact that 40 teachers voluntarily gathered at this inconvenient time provides an indication of the enthusiasm the project had generated at even this early stage of its growth.

CHAPTER FIVE

ITWA and the Schools

SEVERAL times in our report we have run ahead of the story, and this has now happened again. Actually, the Glens Falls program in "Improving the Teaching of World Affairs" started with the opening of the fall term in September, 1957, nearly two months before the Advisory Committee held its first meeting. As a result, the Director of the project had already been confronted with several of the problems which the committee could, and did, note and tried to resolve in its recommendations.

The Director encountered perhaps the most difficult problem during the course of his initial presentation of the project at the opening of the 1957 fall term. As part of the process of launching the trial effort, he visited the different schools to explain the proposal, to display teaching materials and to discuss ways and means with the teachers. He ended his first presentation with the feeling that he had done a satisfactory job. This illusion was quickly punctured when he opened the meeting for discussion. We agree the project is important, the teachers said in effect. We are ready to work with you. We like the suggested materials. Now what do we do?

This was not the response the Director wanted, but he realized that he, not the teachers, was responsible for the misunderstanding. Inadvertently, he had given the impression that the problem of developing a larger awareness of and keener sense of responsibility for world affairs could be solved by a simple formula, by accumulating materials, or perhaps by a new unit of work or a new course of study injected at this or that point in the curriculum.

Convinced that he had started on the wrong track, the Director returned for a second meeting with this same group of teachers. This time he asked the questions. "What are you now doing to develop a world point of view?" he asked. "How can you improve your present efforts? What more can you do?"

The key to the success of the Glens Falls effort depended upon the shifting of the major burden of responsibility from the administration to the classroom teachers. Once this was done, there was still plenty of room for the exercise of educational leadership, and this, too, played a significant role.

Success also depended upon the acceptance by the teachers of the disturbing but undeniable fact that the processes of education can be achieved only by the cumulative impact and continual reinforcement of experience. The chances of success increase immeasurably if the effort is started with the young child and systematically carried on through all the years of schooling.

It is a tribute to the Glens Falls faculty that as a whole the teachers quickly recognized the validity of this point of view and adopted it as a guiding principle in their work with the ITWA program. It would be misleading, however, to pretend that every member of the faculty understood and acted upon this principle. As the Director of Instruction, Robert N. King, pointed out to a reporter several years after the program started, "Some teachers still want to know *what* to teach. They want the security of a neatly organized curriculum and packaged courses of study. But this is a security none of us can hope to have. An activity that works in Glens Falls may not work at all in a different environment, in Harlem or Westchester County, in England or Italy or Japan."[6]

Before the ITWA program began, the responsibility for teaching world affairs in the Glens Falls Schools was limited almost exclusively to the social studies department. To be sure, incidental contributions were made through the teaching of literature, art, music, science, and current affairs, but these were not organized as part of a total school program. Although the teachers of

[6] When the program started in 1957, Mr. King was principal of one of the elementary schools in Glens Falls. From the beginning he exercised leadership in the program, and in the latter years, while serving as Director of Instruction for the school system, he worked closely with the Director of ITWA.

foreign languages, such as French and German, made a significant contribution to the understanding of a single country, or culture, there was no concerted effort to present a total picture of the richness and diversity of the world as a whole. And in the social studies themselves, major emphasis was upon the Western world, or more accurately upon North Atlantic civilization, with only passing reference to Asia, Africa, and Latin America. In short, the teaching of world affairs was an incidental part of instruction in both the elementary and secondary schools. As a consequence, many students finished high school with little, if any, understanding of non-Western cultures; with disorganized and fragmented scraps of information about the contributions of other peoples to world civilization; and with numerous false notions about the position and responsibility of the United States in the world community. Putting it bluntly, these young people approached the duties of adult citizenship with many insular prejudices and only a meager store of the knowledge needed for understanding the problems of a world in turmoil.

This situation began to change the moment teachers accepted their responsibility to improve the teaching of world affairs. Once the individual teacher understood that he had complete freedom to exercise his own originality, reports of "promising practices" began to flow into the ITWA office. The change in outlook, in a point of view, released a previously untapped reservoir of creativity. In the following examples, we get a glimpse of the extent to which the new outlook permeated and influenced every aspect of the curriculum. A more comprehensive sampling of the activities generated by the ITWA Project appears in a later section of this report.

There was the first grade teacher who added a new dimension to her reading lesson. In the past she had used a basic reader in which such words as mother, father, home, work, and play were presented in the context of an upper-middle-class, white, American family. The realization that this presentation might well leave the pupils with distorted concepts prompted the teacher to develop the lesson with a variety of pictures showing families at work and at play in other lands. "Home" took on new meaning to the children, who now understood that it could be an igloo, a hut, a cabin, a farmhouse, or a city apartment, and families around the world became something more than verbal abstractions.

There were the elementary school teachers who began increasingly to identify the stories the children were reading with the country in which the characters lived, and by means of maps and globes and background information related the stories to their locale.

There was the fifth grade class in which the pupils took the initiative in improving their handwriting as the result of an exchange of letters with a fifth grade class in Scotland.

There were the annual fund-raising drives for CARE, for the hospital ship HOPE, and similar causes, sponsored by the student senate in the junior high school and frequently highlighted by original dramatizations for school assembly programs.

There was the mechanical drawing class in which the students developed basic skills by representing a globe on a flat map and then converting the flat map back to a globe.

There was the Speakers Corps in the senior high school which sent out teams of speakers to luncheon clubs and other groups to provide informative thirty-minute discussions of important issues in world affairs.

Although no new courses had been introduced, or even proposed, an international flavor came to permeate the entire curriculum. Teachers who in the introductory stages of the program had tended to divide the subjects in the curriculum into two categories, those that were especially appropriate to develop international understanding and those that were not, began to learn that this was an artificial distinction. Teachers of business education found that there was much to be learned from other countries through comparisons of the forms of business letters, bookkeeping methods, operation of office machines, systems of shorthand and methods of advertising and merchandising. Like others, they realized that the more they learned about different countries, the better they understood their own. Homemaking teachers found that geography added depth to their lessons about food and clothing. Physical education teachers found that children were interested in the similarity of games throughout the world, industrial arts teachers found new meaning in the study of the metric and the British measurement systems. It soon became apparent that there was no subject in the curriculum that could properly be isolated from a world point of view.

These samples, selected almost at random, illustrate the incidental effects produced by a new outlook on the world. One might liken them to sparks flashing from a grinding wheel.

More basic was the deliberate and systematic effort to deepen and broaden understanding of certain key generalizations by providing cumulative experiences from grades one through twelve. Here, too, a few examples will serve as an illustration of the careful planning that went into the program.

Generalization, essentially geographic in nature: "The world is shrinking in distance and time."

A first grade class discovers that a bus ride downtown takes only three minutes, whereas it takes fifteen minutes to walk the same distance.

A third grade class learns that a jet plane can make the ten-week voyage of Columbus in six hours.

A sixth grade class reads that flight over the North Pole brings Moscow as close to Chicago as it is to New York City.

A junior high school class in arithmetic computes the changes involved in flying through several time zones.

A senior high school biology class learns that the outbreak of a tropical disease may be as close as the nearest airport.

Generalization, essentially economic in nature: "Food, clothing, and shelter are basic needs of all human beings."

A first grade class studies homes and foods of children in other lands.

A third grade class studying India uses a film that shows that many people are living on a bare subsistence level, and that this is influencing their health, education, and happiness.

A fifth grade class studies how the wealth and welfare of Norway relate to the way basic human needs are met in food, occupations, shelter, and recreation.

A junior high school class in social studies learns about community dependence on world markets.

A senior high school class in American history debates the question of foreign aid to underdeveloped countries.

A senior high school class in secretarial practice uses motion picture films to learn about free enterprise systems in various countries.

Generalization, essentially social in nature: "A knowledge of cultures of other nations contributes to better communication and international understanding."

A second grade class learns some of the songs sung by French school children.

A physical education class learns to dance the *kolo*, or *sieben schrutt*.

A fourth grade class studies the contributions of European scientists to American science, and vice versa.

A sixth grade class makes a list of American words derived from foreign languages.

A junior high school class in physical education learns the meaning of "football" in the United States and in Europe.

A junior high school assembly enjoys a program of Nigerian music and dancing.

A junior high school class in homemaking compares life in North and South America.

A senior high school class in world history compiles a list of Nobel Prize winners in science.

A senior high school class in English reads from a list of novels about life in Asia.

Generalization, essentially political in nature: "The recognition of human rights and human dignity is basic to personal relationships and to government."

A second grade class learns to settle a dispute, to analyze the cause of the argument, and to arrive at a fair decision.

A fourth grade class learns to organize itself into a democratic group and to elect officers.

A fifth grade class studies the United Nations Declaration of Human Rights.

A sixth grade class compares the rights and responsibilities of a citizen of the Soviet Union with those of a citizen of the United States.

A junior high school social studies class compares the preamble of the United States Constitution with the preamble of the United Nations Charter.

A junior high school Pen Pal Club prepares an exhibit of postage stamps.

A senior high school physical education class studies the effects of the Cold War on the Olympic Games.

A senior high school World Affairs Club conducts a model session of the United Nations Security Council and invites other schools to participate.

At this point we pause to anticipate a question that became all too familiar to those who undertook to explain the ITWA program during the early period of its development. "This is interesting, but what's new about it? We (it is a teacher who is speaking) have been doing this for years."

The answer to the question—and to the *ex cathedra* comment —is that there is all the difference in the world between a meaningful activity and the same activity when it lacks direction and purpose, either in the mind of the teacher or the pupil, or both.

In his classic film, *The Plow that Broke the Plains*, Charles Flaherty begins a powerful story with a rainstorm in the Appalachian Mountains. We see the separate drops of water falling on the soil and dislodging grains of sand and small pebbles. Then, as the story gains momentum, we see the raindrops merging into tiny rivulets, rivulets combining to form streams, streams flowing into brooks, brooks emptying into creeks, creeks pouring into rivers, and rivers swollen to mighty torrents bursting their banks and surging with irresistible force into the Mississippi and down to the sea.

Such in its own way is the Glens Falls story. Or, rather, part of the story, for the classroom activities represent only one category of the many interrelated aspects of the program.

The ITWA office became a communications and coordinating center for all these activities. The Director served as counselor, consultant, librarian, custodian of films and filmstrips and recordings, head of publicity, host to visitors, and liaison between the ITWA program and the community.

As the experiment gathered headway, teachers, working individually or in groups, began to transform "promising practices" into lesson plans, new units of work, and revised courses of study. This development led to requests for new instructional materials, including maps, student newspapers, news magazines, newspapers and periodicals, books and reference works of all kinds. To meet these requests, the Director and his staff compiled bibliographies, previewed films and filmstrips and recordings, located new material, and secured exhibits. The first exhibit came from Zurich, Switzerland. It consisted of a representative collection, drawn from several European countries, of art work created by students between the ages of seven and seventeen. When it was returned several months later, the ITWA Project sent with it an exhibit of art from the Glens Falls schools.

The collection of reference materials in the ITWA office soon reached sizable dimensions. In addition to several daily and classroom periodicals and weekly news magazines, it included a number of newspapers from other lands, among them the *Hindu Weekly Review*, the *Swiss Review of World Affairs*, the *Manchester Guardian*, as well as *Great Decisions* of the Foreign Policy Association and the *World Affairs Guide* of the Minneapolis *Star*. It also included relevant books, pamphlets, and periodicals, among them the UNESCO *Courier*, *Focus* of the American Geographical Society, and the *Bulletin* of the Foreign Policy Association. For a time, the central library of instructional materials proved adequate, but as the project grew it became necessary to establish separate collections in each of the schools. The value of the effort to meet the demands for supplementary materials and to make them readily available cannot be overestimated.

Requests for lectures, workshops, and other means whereby teachers could update and advance their own education also reached the Director's office in growing numbers. The administration made every effort to meet these requests. It became clear that teacher education was, perhaps, the most significant and outstanding of the many benefits the ITWA Project brought to the school system.

Since the development of in-service education was a matter of immediate and direct concern to the Glens Falls Teachers Association, a few words about this organization are relevant. The staff of the seven schools (one senior high school, one junior high school, and five elementary schools), some 200 teachers and administrators, is the instructional arm of the Board of Education. But the staff is also organized as a professional group, known as the Teachers Association, with a membership of from 98 to 100 percent of the faculty. To say that this is a more or less meaningless distinction is to overlook the motivation of a professional group which sometimes accepts, sometimes initiates, recommendations for improvements in instruction, curriculum, and the welfare of its members. We shall have more to say about the role of the

Teachers Association in the ITWA Project in a later section of this report. The point made here is that the extensive program of in-service education the World Affairs Project set in motion owed much of its success to the planning and support of this professional organization.

During the 1957-1958 school year, five workshops were devoted to the ITWA program. Conducted by specialists and attended by from 25 to 50 teachers, these two and one half- to three-hour sessions were devoted to a consideration of the following subjects: "Basic Principles of Constructing Evaluation Instruments"; "Looking at the Elementary Curriculum"; "Geography in World Affairs"; "The World Comes Into the Classroom"; and, in a session held late in May, "Evaluating the ITWA Program." In this, the final workshop of the first year, the teachers undertook in the light of the year's experience to revise the "orientation" statement the ITWA Advisory Committee had drafted at the beginning of the school year. In later years and other workshops, the teachers explored the relationship between ITWA and the various subjects in the curriculum.

Encouraged by the attendance at these workshops, the ITWA subcommittee organized a seven-day conference for the week immediately following the close of school. The conference, devoted to the subject of geography, was held at an attractive campsite on the shores of Lake George with about thirty teachers in attendance. The success of the venture prompted the ITWA subcommittee to organize similar conferences in 1959 and 1960, the first on the theme of "The Nature of the Non-Western World," the second on the subject of "World Health."

Incidentally, the Teachers Association reaped a rich dividend from its share of the organization and support of the June conferences. At the end of the first conference, the camp owners agreed to an arrangement whereby the members of the Glens Falls Teachers Association could use the camp facilities during the out-of-season months of June and September.

The Teachers Association and the ITWA subcommittee also cooperated on in-service courses for teachers during the school year. During the first year of ITWA, and independent of it, the Association arranged a 30-hour course for local in-service credit but without college credit. The course on the history of the Glens Falls community was given by the retired Superintendent of Schools, A. W. Miller. In the spring of 1960 the Professional Growth Committee of the Teachers Association received requests for a course to be given by Dr. Yu-kuang Chu, chairman of the Oriental Studies Department at nearby Skidmore College in Saratoga Springs. By joint arrangement with the ITWA office, Dr. Chu was invited to give a survey course on "Asian Cultures." More than 50 teachers, some from surrounding communities, attended the fifteen two-hour sessions.

In addition to the more conventional types of in-service training, the ITWA office provided opportunities for travel. For example, each year on Columbus Day, a school holiday, the ITWA office sponsored a visit by teachers to the United Nations. The group, numbering annually about twelve, toured the United Nations Building, met in briefing sessions with a staff member of the Department of Public Information, and visited the World Affairs Center across the street from the U. N. for additional briefing sessions.

The ITWA office also provided an opportunity each year for a group of teachers up to ten in number to spend their spring vacations in Washington. With their travel expenses paid out of ITWA funds, the teachers visited the National Education Association, the National Geographic Society, the Pan-American Union, the Washington International Center, and various government offices and embassies. The Curriculum Materials Laboratory in the U. S. Office of Education, which served as headquarters for the group, provided guidance and assistance to the teachers in the form of specialists in both curriculum and subject matter.

Although the ITWA office was in no position to provide funds for overseas travel, it did help to open this opportunity to interested teachers. In cooperation with the Experiment in International Living and other organizations, the ITWA staff assisted teachers in their arrangements for travel to other countries. One elementary school music teacher joined a theater and music festival tour. A junior high school teacher went to Nigeria as a Community Ambassador. High school teachers served as tour directors for groups going to Germany, to India, and to Japan.

Other teachers traveled to Mexico, Alaska, and various European countries.

Meanwhile, travelers from other parts of the United States and from overseas were making their way to Glens Falls. We noted earlier that between 1957 and 1962 more than 200 visitors from 60 different countries came to Glens Falls for visits lasting from a day to several weeks or months. Most of these visitors traveled under the auspices of agencies, both public and private, engaged in exchange-of-persons programs. Among these are the American Field Service Committee, the Experiment in International Living, the Governmental Affairs Institute, the New York Herald Tribune High School Forum, the Institute of International Education, and the Office of Education of the U. S. Department of Health, Education, and Welfare. In addition, several foreign embassies have cooperated by sending cultural officers, in one case an Ambassador, to participate in school programs. In one instance a teacher from the Mayfield School in London visited Glens Falls High School because of an exchange of correspondence between typewriting classes in the two schools.

The majority of these visitors came ostensibly to observe schools and community life, particularly because of the ITWA program. The opportunity could not be overlooked, however, to invite the visitors to share in class discussion, to address assembly groups, and otherwise to participate in school activities. Here the philosophy of the ITWA program became indisputably clear. Geography, history, and language classes were not alone in wishing to share the time and attention of the visitors. Homemaking, business, music, art, physical education, and other classes were equally eager to have a portion of a visitor's time. The visitors, for their part, were more than willing to cooperate. As teachers, which most of them were, they were articulate before classes and alert to the common interests of students the world over. One Japanese teacher, Mr. Sawamura, who planned originally for a one- or two-day visit to a third grade classroom became so interested that he stayed nearly two weeks!

Not all the visitors were adults. Many were teen-age students visiting this country under the auspices of the Herald Tribune Forum, the American Field Service Committee, and similar organizations. But, like the older travelers, these young people made an enthusiastic contribution to the school program.

It would be impossible to overestimate the impact of visitors from other lands upon the schools and the community. No one in Glens Falls would disagree with the conclusion expressed by one teacher that "the reception of visitors has been one of the outstanding and rewarding experiences of the ITWA program for students and teachers alike."

Nor would anyone in either the school or the community be likely to disagree with the verdict of one of the high school students. The student, a girl, had written a favorable review of several novels about Asia she had read in her English class. Not content to leave the matter at this point, she went on to add by way of conclusion:

"These books are interesting and develop our concept of a country's culture and background, but they don't make the people any more real. It takes exchange students to do this. I doubt if I will ever forget the Chinese girl, Yeng. We invited her to our installation of the new Hi-Y members. Here we wanted her to become an honorary member. At this point she began to cry. We were terrified for fear we had offended her, or perhaps she couldn't join because the pledge mentioned Christian character. It was nothing so drastic that had caused the tears. She felt she didn't deserve anything so wonderful! In voicing this opinion we believe that she did deserve it more than anyone in the club. If we had understood her more as she comprehended how much it meant for her to be accepted to the Hi-Y, we would not have thought we had offended her.

"Anyway, Yeng made the story-book characters live. Possibly the next Chinese person I meet may be disagreeable, but no matter how much so, he will never destroy the favorable impression Yeng has left with me."[7]

---

[7] Quoted from Mabelle E. McNulty, "Report from Glens Falls," *Social Education*, May, 1961, p. 226.

CHAPTER SIX

ITWA and the Community

T HE World Affairs Project launched in Glens Falls in the autumn of 1957 was designed as a three-year trial effort to end with the close of the school year in June 1960. In 1963, more than six years after it started, the project was still going on, but no longer on a trial basis. The Board of Education by unanimous vote had decided to incorporate the World Affairs office into the existing structure of the school system and to make the temporary organization into a permanent one. With this decision, the Board placed the ultimate stamp of community approval upon the project.

An editorial in the Glens Falls *Post-Star* for December 10, 1960, expressed community confidence in more eloquent, if less concrete, terms. "One of the advantages of doing a pilot project like this is what we ourselves learn. Over the period of the experiment a list of visitors reading like a United Nations roll call has been compiled in the Glens Falls schools. It is composed of foreign teachers, students, diplomats, and at least one politician. Many were guests in local homes.

"Glens Falls students learned from them and they, we are entitled to believe, found something memorable in Glens Falls. In the end though, the principal result of this project must be the stimulus it gives American education to bring the world into our classrooms and relate our country to it."

The world did indeed come into Glens Falls classrooms in a new and significant way as a result of the ITWA program. At the same time, the students were projected beyond the walls of the school and the confines of the small town and out upon a stage that was

38

as broad as the earth. Meanwhile, the community itself was transformed.

The transformation of the community was not an accidental— or, for that matter, even an incidental—consequence of the organized effort to develop a keener awareness of and knowledge about world affairs. It was, rather, the product of a deliberate plan to build an educational program into both the schools and the community.

Shortly after the ITWA program got under way the Director of the project, acting upon the authorization of the Board of Education, invited city officials, representatives of service clubs and civic associations, members of the Parent-Teachers Association, and other interested citizens to a public meeting. After a discussion of the aims of the newly launched pilot study, those attending the meeting formed a Citizen's Committee for ITWA with the city librarian as chairman. The committee agreed to serve as a liaison agency. As part of its responsibility, it agreed to keep the channels of communication open, to assist in the entertainment of overseas visitors, and to help coordinate activities involving both the schools and the community.

Ties between the schools and the community were also strengthened through the direct coordination of the ITWA program and projects in international education carried on by organizations such as the Red Cross, the Girl Scouts, the Rotary Club, the Junior Chamber of Commerce, and the Glens Falls Committee for the United Nations. Through the Red Cross, especially its Junior Chapter, the schools were able to borrow exhibits from other countries and to send contributions of food, clothing, and educational materials to needy areas of the world. Leaders of the Girl Scouts developed programs designed to supplement and strengthen the work being carried on in the schools. The Rotary Club shared the expenses of lectures on world affairs, helped establish pen pal programs, and sponsored contests in which prizes were awarded to high school seniors for distinguished achievement in designated aspects of the ITWA program.

One of the immediate gains from the systematic effort to strengthen school-community cooperation was the revitalization of the Community Ambassador Project, an affiliate of the Experiment in International Living. In this project, which in 1957-1958 was being sponsored by the Junior Chamber of Commerce, two young people from Glens Falls traveled abroad each summer as "Community Ambassadors" with all expenses paid. The project, which had been going on for more than a decade, provided Glens Falls with a rich source of information and experience waiting to be tapped for the ITWA program. And it was tapped. The former "Community Ambassadors" formed an organization and agreed to accept a portion of the responsibility for welcoming overseas visitors, and to share their experiences with students through classroom visits and in other ways the ITWA staff might suggest.

The Glens Falls Committee for the United Nations, organized to promote the cause of the U. N. and open to all interested citizens, also formed an important link in the chain of school-community cooperation. Operating on a budget contributed by business and other organizations, the committee has promoted the annual observance of United Nations Day, organized the Hallowe'en "Trick-or-Treat" coin collection for the United Nations Children's Emergency Fund, and sold U. N. Christmas cards. As another continuing activity, the committee has each spring sent a delegation of high school juniors to a seminar on the United Nations conducted in New York by the American Friends Service Committee.

The information services of both the school and the community provided another essential link in the chain of cooperation. From the beginning, the two local newspapers—*The Glen Falls Times* and *The Post-Star*—worked closely with the ITWA office. Photographers and news reporters were always on hand to cover the arrival of guests and to report newsworthy programs. Editorial support was consistently strong.

But the major responsibility for informing the public about the World Affairs program rested, as it rightly should, upon the schools themselves. In addition to news items prepared in the ITWA office and published in the local press, information reached the community through *The School Bell*, a printed publication sponsored by the Teachers Association and the Board of Education. The ITWA office distributed two occasional publications. One, titled *ITWA's Expressly So*, kept the faculty informed of the latest developments in the program. The other, a *Newsletter* distributed two or three times each year, served as an informal report to friends, benefactors, and people in other communities throughout the country who had expressed an interest in the program.

The matters of organization and mechanics we have been outlining are not, however, the essential part of the story. News is really news only when it brings something "fresh" and "new" to the reader, and this situation exists only when the reader himself recognizes that he is personally involved and immediately concerned with the subject under discussion.

It is impossible to say which aspect of the rich and varied program did the most to arouse in the community an awareness of the larger world beyond its immediate boundaries. Most obvious, of course, was the impact of visitors from other countries. As the program developed, the community as a whole looked forward to the arrival of guests from other lands, and families vied with each other for the privilege of entertaining the visitors. The depth of the personal involvement is revealed, at least in some small measure, in the following letters, written to the Director of ITWA after a delegation of educators from Eritrea had spent several days in Glens Falls.

The first letter:

"I should like you to know," the writer began, "how very pleasant the past week has been with Mr. Kahsai as our guest. It was one of the most wonderful experiences our family has ever had.

"The week went by too fast, and Mr. Kahsai indicated he felt the same way and looks forward to the time he might be able to visit with us again. In the interim, I expect we shall be corresponding.

"What my children, my husband, and I gained from Mr. Kahsai's visit is almost impossible to put into words. We gained a deep insight from his views into many of our ways of living that we take for granted. Likewise, we were impressed with his description of 'common' ways of family living in Eritrea, ways quite different from ours.

"Thank you again for giving us this opportunity, and please do not forget us in the future."

The second letter:

". . . I believe our guest gained a completely different view of American life from the one he held when he arrived in Glens Falls. We, too, learned that Eritrea is more than a strip of land attached to Ethiopia, as the map shows us.

"This was a lesson in mutual understanding. Our ways and our colors are different, but our basic problems are similar—how best to educate our young . . . . (Our guest) was much impressed by the easy relationship here between husband and wife, a relationship which cannot exist in his country, since women have not yet attained full status. I have a feeling he will be more amenable to equality for women after this visit.

"It was a most gratifying experience. We hope more Americans will open their homes to visitors from overseas. They need our help and understanding and we need theirs."

A third letter:

"His reaction to American life was a lesson in itself. He adjusted to it beautifully, seizing every opportunity to learn without surrendering an ounce of his own individuality, dignity, or pride in his own culture.

"His skill in language (including at least a passing familiarity with English, Italian, Arabic, Amharic, and several Eritrean languages or dialects) emphasized to us the narrowness of the linguistic training most of us received in school, and the need for American schools of today to improve in this regard.

"One other lesson driven home to us was the scarcity of educational facilities in Eritrea and, we would surmise, in Africa generally. In a vague sort of way we were aware of this. Still, coming face to face with the intense desire of these people to improve their schools, and learning from them the basic problems, such as shortage of teachers and shortage of textbooks in an appropriate language, we came to a heightened realization of something we should always remember, there is a tremendous amount which we Americans can accomplish with foreign aid of a strictly non-material nature."

The visitors from other lands, more than 200 from 60 countries in the years from 1957 to 1962, left an indelible impression upon the Glens Falls community, school and town alike. But so, too, in a much less dramatic but equally influential way did the day-by-day effort to bring the world into the classroom and the community. No one in any walk of life could escape for very long from the reminder that the children and youths in the schools were being confronted daily with the challenge to understand and accept their responsibilities as members of the human family. In its own quiet way, the search for larger meaning, for understanding, which went on in every school and in a variety of activities in many classrooms, was perhaps as influential in modifying prejudices and sharpening social sensitivity as the much more dramatic impact of the visitors from abroad. The result was a quickened interest in and awareness of world affairs in both school and community. As the program developed, the schools stimulated the community and the community, in turn, stimulated the schools to further efforts.

Examples of the initiative taken by the community could be multiplied many times. Two—one involving the World Affairs Council of Citizens, the other a local chapter of the DAR—speak for themselves.

In the spring of 1958 the World Affairs Council invited a group of 14 overseas college students studying in the Albany area to Glens Falls for a three-day visit. The Council arranged housing, tours, and entertainment for the students. It also sponsored an "International Friendship Festival" in which through songs, stories, and dances the students gave their interpretation of several different national cultures. Money raised from the sale of tickets for the festival paid the expenses of bringing the students to Glens Falls, and there was enough left over to give the 14 young visiting students a trip to New York.

At about the same time as the World Affairs Council was showing young people from other countries to Glens Falls, the Chepontuc Chapter of the Daughters of the American Revolution sent its delegate, Mrs. William E. Montgomery, to Washington. Delegate Montgomery went to the Continental Congress with instructions from her chapter to oppose any DAR resolutions opposing the

United Nations. Five years before another Glens Falls delegate, Mrs. Philip R. Peck, had had to stand alone and vote "No" on an anti-U.N. resolution. In 1958 Mrs. Montgomery was one of 75 in the convention of 2,000 to oppose a similar resolution. In an editorial congratulating Delegate Montgomery for her stand, *The Berkshire Eagle* thanked her for "jabbing the organization's national leadership with a hatpin of logic."

In this particular instance, the DAR incident and the ITWA program were related only in the sense that they shared a common objective. This was true of other activities carried on in the community during the course of the experiment. Certainly some of these activities, perhaps most, would have taken place even if there had been no ITWA program in the schools. But at worst they would have gone relatively unnoticed by most of the community, and at best they would have attracted the attention of only the small groups of citizens immediately involved. The ITWA program brought all the activities into focus and set in motion a process of interaction which fed upon itself.

Beneath the more dramatic developments, such as the DAR Chapter's stand on the United Nations and the "International Friendship Festival" sponsored by the World Affairs Council of Citizens, were the day-by-day activities and incidents in town and school—exhibits jointly sponsored by school and town libraries; speakers brought to the town by service clubs, civic organizations, and churches; the cooperation of the business community in the form of tours through the plants, information and advice, and visits to the schools to speak to and counsel with the students. Taken separately, none of these activities stands out as especially important. Their significance lies in the cumulative effect they had upon students and adults alike—in brief, upon the entire community.

Those who have been closest to the Glens Falls Project are quick to assert that the most valuable result of the venture has been its influence upon the community at large. Unfortunately, the assertion must remain debatable for there is no evidence that can be put to the test on a computer.

One who wishes to defend the proposition can, however, produce a wealth of testimony from the townspeople. He can cite the financial support that came from various sources in the community when, in the middle of the three-year program, the effort was in danger of withering on the vine for lack of funds. And he can advance the persuasive argument that when the pilot study as such came to an official conclusion at the end of three years, the Board of Education agreed unanimously that the effort to improve the teaching of world affairs should be continued as an integral part of the educational program.

CHAPTER SEVEN

A Sample of Activities

WORLD affairs is an all-encompassing concept which embraces the totality of mankind's experiences, past and present. Before so vast a concept can be taught in the classroom, it has to be broken down to manageable size. This is the responsibility of teachers and administrators.

The total responsibility for determining what to teach and at what grade level cannot be shifted to the shoulders of the individual classroom teacher. This is as true for world affairs as for every other important concept taught in the schools. Only careful cooperative planning by teachers and administrators will prevent unintentional omissions and needless duplication.

The Glens Falls program was organized around four primary goals: (1) *increasing* understanding of world affairs; (2) *developing* an appreciation of other peoples and cultures; (3) *inculcating* an attitude of respect toward foreign peoples; and (4) *promoting* a sense of responsibility for furthering better understanding of foreign peoples and cultures. The program provided a variety of activities and experiences, each of which was related insofar as possible to the age level and ability of the pupils and to the regular school program.

The following descriptions provide a sampling of learning activities carried on in various grades and in various school subjects from kindergarten through grade 12 as part of the Glens Falls Project on "Improving the Teaching of World Affairs." These were carefully planned as part of the "regular" program for a given grade or course. Most were classroom activities. Others were carried on as extraclassroom activities. Several culminated

46

in assembly programs for other classes or for the entire school. In the latter cases parents frequently attended the programs. All of these activities illustrate ways in which instruction reflected a world point of view.

For easy reference, the remainder of this chapter is divided into four sections dealing with (1) primary, (2) intermediate, (3) junior high, and (4) senior high school levels. There is not space to describe, even briefly, all of the activities which were undertaken as part of the project. Therefore, at the end of each section, a simple list of further activities is provided to give some idea of the scope and sequence of the total experiment.

While the activities mentioned were carried out in the grade indicated, it is recognized that their value may not be restricted to a particular grade. Teachers will find it possible to adapt the activities ascribed to a particular level to classes at other grade levels. It is believed that the activities given will stimulate the development of numerous other activities in teaching an understanding of world affairs.

KINDERGARTEN THROUGH GRADE THREE

The kindergarten is essentially a place for story-telling and game-playing. Under the guidance of the teacher these activities may include role-playing, a highly effective means of understanding another person's outlook. In a Broad Street School kindergarten class the teacher read to the class, "Ting Ling and Mee Too," by Keto, which she found in an old story book. The children sought the book out again and again. As a result more books of Chinese stories were offered. The outcome of this sustained interest was the joint planning of a unit of study, entitled "Our Chinese Friends."

Story books were collected from all possible sources. Two simple filmstrips, albeit about Japanese children, were found and viewed. An art frieze, "Tommy and Dee Dee," was made, comparing "Tommy's Way" and "Dee Dee's Way." Other activities included the preparation of table exhibits on the same theme, the construction of simple objects like kites, lanterns, a "winter bed," and even the making of a crude globe of papier-mache. Cultural comparisons included nursery rhymes, games, songs, simple dances, and holidays known to Tommy or Dee Dee. As a culmination the children created a play which was presented to parents and to all primary grade children in the school.

Meanwhile, in the Kensington Road School, a first grade class entertained a visiting teacher from Japan. After he had answered many of their questions about life in Japan he taught a lesson in paper-folding to show how Japanese children made birds and other likenesses from paper. This led the class teacher to read such stories as Halliday's "Tashio and Tama" and Yashimi's "The Village Tree."

From this interest the children were led to bring from home pictures, post cards, stamps, money, toys, dolls, articles of clothing, dishes, chopsticks and other artifacts of Japanese life. The teacher expressed amazement at the variety. Using the material brought in, she was able to point out both similarities and differences between American and Japanese ways of living. The interest did not lag. Filmstrips such as "Togo and Muki of Japan" (Eye Gate); "Japan: Country Life"; "City Life" (McGraw-Hill); "Japan: Our School Life" (Ohio State University) were procured and used to advantage. In the meantime, a third grade class in the same school was developing a tape-recording exchange program with a third grade class in a Japanese school.

This third grade program had begun, prior to the visit of the Japanese teacher, through the Glens Falls teacher's effort to teach concepts of distance and direction by using simple class-made maps. Out of the concept of "faraway" came a student-expressed wish to exchange information with a "faraway" school. The class voted "Japan" as a faraway place. At first, language differences appeared to the teacher and the ITWA Director as an obstacle to communication. After an inquiry to the Office of Education, Washington, D. C., however, correspondence was quickly established with the Campus School at the University of Hiroshima where UNESCO had provided tape recorders and where elementary teachers were able to translate English into Japanese and vice versa. This led to an exchange of tape recordings which included songs, descriptions of games, and other topics of mutual interest. Soon the two third grade classes were exchanging snapshots, student art work, examples of Japanese brush work, Japanese character-writing, and examples of American penmanship. The teacher at Kensington Road School discovered the technique of making original filmstrips in her own classroom. It was from these exchanges that the aforementioned first grade class was able to borrow specimens of student art. This Japanese-American exchange has been sustained since 1960. Today, however, it involves cooperation with other schools and other teachers in Japan. Even the high school became involved by helping a high school in Kochi with an English-language culture exhibit. Because the program at Kensington Road has continued, the fourth, fifth, and sixth grade students have come back to their third grade teacher to hear the latest tape recordings which arrive two or three times a year from Japan.

By way of evaluation the following comments may be cited. *From parents:* "I didn't realize kindergartners could learn so much"; "I learned a lot myself, listening to Betty tell me things about Dee Dee." *From other teachers:* "Comparing was such a good way to do the unit"; " Even my third-graders learned a lot." *From children:* "They must be very poor if they don't have tractors"; (about reading and writing) "Hey, they're doing it backwards, but they'd say our way was backwards! If I went to live with Dee Dee I'd have to learn Chinese. . . . I'm glad we have an alphabet."

In a second grade at Sanford Street School the boys and girls made original drawings in their art class for Thanksgiving. They expressed a desire to share these and arrangements were made to send them to a second grade class in Pontarlier, France. At Christmas time the Sanford Street class received, in return, a set of hand-drawn Christmas cards from the second grade class in Pontarlier. This whetted their interest to read and learn more about France. The teacher's efforts were aided by the work of the "helping teacher," a reading specialist in the school, who had compiled a catalogue of stories in their readers, classified by countries and geographical areas.

These listings eventually were extended to cover all the readers used in grades three through six and included hundreds of stories. The work of listing these stories by country of cultural origin was begun in a one-week workshop in late June sponsored by the

ITWA program for Glens Falls teachers. Once made, these lists could be easily kept up-to-date. They were circulated among all the elementary schools which could then requisition desired titles from the central book room. This in no way diverted the reading program from its appropriate purpose, nor did it require additional class time to relate the reading instruction to a world viewpoint.

Additional projects, or variations of the above, for grades K through three, include the following:

1. Find out about different ways of eating (fingers, forks, and chopsticks), dressing, working, playing, traveling, and going to school.
2. Collect and discuss pictures, objects and songs from other lands.
3. Study the influence of climate and natural resources on the food, clothing, and shelter of people in other lands.
4. Learn dances and music of foreign lands. Learn a few foreign expressions.
5. Map school or home area. Locate countries on a globe.
6. Learn simple principles of self-government. Learn to make rules.
7. Study the work of UNICEF.
8. Study the family backgrounds of the class. Trace ancestors to other lands.
9. Construct puppets to act out situations involving attitudes of respect toward different people.
10. Support the UNICEF milk fund, Red Cross, or overseas project.
11. Compare various celebrations of holidays and festivals.

INTERMEDIATE GRADES, FOUR THROUGH SIX

An interest in music and in folk dancing of other lands has been developed in the upper grades of the Jackson Heights School. With the aid of a music supervisor, a classroom teacher has produced annually a series of original glee club programs based on the study of a given cultural area or on an imaginary round-the-world trip. In each program members of the glee club described for the audience the cultural significance of the songs.

Another teacher at Jackson Heights School has used a series of recordings by Michael Herman as well as various pamphlets to develop programs of folk dances with her fifth grade classes. One of these programs developed into an assembly program which included folk dances from several countries. "The Virginia Reel" was used to represent the United States. Mexico was interpreted through the "Hat Dance." Using *Fun Around the World* (Women's Guild of the United Nations), the class found information to create a scene on Judica, a Czech holiday, which provided an opportunity to dance "The Wheat." The Danish dance, "The Seven Jumps," was related to a pre-Lenten celebration of Shrove Tuesday. A Hebrew calendar provided information about the Israeli "Hora," a dance associated with the theme of Israel's independence day in May. Costumes were kept simple. Decorations, including flags, were authentic.

More recently another teacher at Jackson Heights School produced a Polish folk dance festival for an assembly. By popular request it was repeated for a P.T.A. program.

Two sixth grade teachers, representing Sanford Street and Kensington Road Schools, collaborated to develop a systematic program for teaching current world affairs. Their stated aims included: acquainting their students with news magazines and newspapers; developing a knowledge of special situations in the world which receive headline attention; distinguishing between fact and opinion; sustaining interest in continued reading about the topics discussed in class. Individual reports, committee reports, and bulletin board displays based on news stories were included in the methods used. As results of this program teachers were asked to provide more periodicals for reading and parents commented on a new reading interest at home. One child was heard to say: "I don't read the funny page first any more, I read the front page." Improvement was observed in reading, writing, speaking, and listening.

The presence of a fifth grade exchange teacher from Oslo, Norway, at Big Cross Street School, the year before the ITWA program was launched, created an interest in Europe and European schools which has not diminished. One class followed vicariously the travels through Europe of the teacher's daughter who visited the former exchange teacher in Oslo as well as other friends of the ITWA program in Luxembourg and England. This was a "people-to-people" program in action. It has been reflected in art, music, social studies and the language arts. The P.T.A. unit in this school, as in others, has sponsored food festivals, dance programs, and other cultural exchanges in its own programs. An extensive pen pal correspondence at Broad Street School was reported regularly to the school by means of pinpointing on a world map the places to and from which letters had been sent and received.

As the ITWA program has developed, emphasis has been placed on developing a world point of view in every school, grade, and subject. Every workshop for teachers and every curriculum committee has included representatives from various grades and subjects. Overseas visitors have met with pupils and teachers in all grades, K-12. The imagination and ingenuity of the teachers and administrators have been the sole limiting factors in the program. The thinking of the faculty has been stretched to provide more ideas and methods for improving instruction about the world and its peoples. The domain of world affairs is "what the people of the world think, feel and do."

Additional projects, or variations of the above, for *grades four, five and six* include the following:

1. Study the world in terms of geographical and cultural regions, relating climate and geography to the lives of the people.
2. Emphasize the study of world affairs through intensive reading programs.
3. Study and prepare displays to illustrate the artistic and cultural growth of countries.
4. Develop map skills, including familiarity with map projections, latitude, longitude, and time zones.
5. Build vocabulary of foreign words and expressions; start formal study of languages where possible.
6. Continue and deepen the study of the principles and organs of the U. N.
7. Relate the study of current events to the historical events of a country.
8. Study an overseas country in depth; consider basic problems of food, health, soil and resource conservation, etc.; compare with the U. S.
9. Trace the dependence of the United States on other countries for such items as foods, natural resources, and trained minds.
10. Exchange letters, booklets, pictures, or tape recordings with classes overseas.
11. Learn the various kinds of coins of foreign countries. Make collections of coins—or cothing, dolls, pottery, or artifacts from other countries.

12. Conduct meetings, elect officers, and make group decisions.
13. Study problems relating to racial and ethnic differences.
14. Study the rights and responsibilities of people as found in the U. S. Constitution, U.N. Charter, Universal Declaration of Human Rights and other documents of this kind.
15. Study the flags and their histories (from all countries, including U. S.).
16. Provide for overseas visitors to our schools and homes; learn to ask questions which reflect our concern for other peoples.
17. Continue support of overseas projects such as UNICEF, Red Cross and CARE.
18. Arrange class festivals, assembly programs, dinners, bazaars with an overseas country as a theme.

JUNIOR HIGH SCHOOL

In the junior high school the ITWA program has reached from classroom to classroom to become school-wide. One of the teachers, who had been a Community Ambassador to Nigeria, inspired a committee of teachers to plan jointly an "Accent on Africa" program for the 1959-1960 school year. The committee included an English teacher, a homemaking teacher, a social studies teacher, a science teacher, a music teacher, a librarian, and a helping teacher. The year-long program, which culminated in an interscholastic conference for ninth-graders, included the study of literature, food, family life, science-resource materials, music, and sculpture in the emerging African nations. Assembly programs presented African students and diplomats, as well as performing artists who interpreted African culture.

An important facet of school life in the junior high school is the preparation of the newspaper, *Junior Highlights*. Each year 35 or more students on the staff of the paper attend the school journalism conference at Columbia University. As part of their trip, the group visits the United Nations. Following one of these trips a group of students wrote and produced a play for the school's observance of U.N. Day on October 24. The play, entitled "A Space Man's Visit to U.N. Headquarters," portrayed the work of the main organs and the specialized agencies of the U.N., as seen and interpreted by junior high school students. Needless to say, *Junior Highlights* reports all ITWA activities in the school. The sponsor of *Junior Highlights*, Mabelle McNulty, contributed an article, "Report From Glens Falls," which appeared in *Social Education* for May 1961.

Other junior high school programs have been built on such themes as "Look at Latin America," and "Eyes on Europe." Homemaking classes have studied meal preparation and family care. Social studies teachers have aided, and been aided by, teachers of other subjects as appropriate themes and topics emerged in more than a single class or grade. The librarian has prepared a special catalogue for her own use in answering the many requests of students and teachers for information on special topics. A description of this catalogue "The World In A Box" by Mary Renaud was published in *Wilson Library Bulletin* for November 1959.

In addition, the following projects or activities were attempted by one or more of the classes in *grades seven through nine:*

1. Continue the study of maps and map projections to include Mercator, Polar centered, and Interrupted or "Orange Peel" types.
2. Develop lists or essays on: newly independent nations, overseas imports and exports to and from this community; marriage and courting customs of other countries; scientific discoveries by foreigners; etc.
3. Maintain wall maps for current events, or to illustrate such things as the major language areas of the world.
4. Keep a card index of books read about life in other lands.
5. Present talks to classes or assemblies by foreign students, or by youngsters who have traveled to other countries.
6. Arrange for a concert as an assembly program by a musician from another cultural area; prepare "program notes" on nationality and background of composers.
7. Continue foreign language study, including songs, folk stories, etc.
8. Plan an intercultural festival (foods, music, or dances) as a P.T.A. program.
9. Collect travel posters, pamphlets and information sheets prepared by other countries.
10. Use editorials reflecting disagreement on a given issue as a basis for class discussion.
11. Form clubs or hobby groups for: foreign foods, pen pal correspondence, stamp collecting, collections of art, coins, etc.
12. Compile a list of dietary rules or observances by various religious groups.

13. Develop a simple rating scale to judge the achievement of various countries in fulfilling the Universal Declaration of Human Rights.
14. Maintain the various fund-raising activities for overseas relief.
15. Help prepare library or corridor exhibits of pictures, stamps, coins, etc.
16. Write articles for the school newspaper about overseas visitors, classroom or assembly programs on world affairs.
17. Prepare daily news digest for use over the P.A. system, stressing news of science, art, literature, music, business, drama, health, food, as well as politics and international relations.
18. Prepare tape recordings describing home, school, and community life in the U. S. for exchange with schools in other countries.
19. Arrange to exchange newspapers with an overseas student.
20. Arrange to interview a local businessman to discuss the relation of his business to the world market.

SENIOR HIGH SCHOOL

World affairs activities in the senior high school have been as wide and as varied as the curriculum itself. Each department has found its own way to enrich and improve instruction by developing a world affairs viewpoint. Perhaps the best way of illustrating what has been done is to provide a brief summary for each subject.

Art. In senior high school art classes, as also in the other schools, the students benefited from the exchange of exhibits of student art work with a collection center in Zurich, Switzerland. For their part the Glens Falls students drew travel posters and other pictures depicting the American scene.

Business Education. Classes in shorthand and typing exchanged model business letters with a high school in London. They learned not only about differences in the shorthand systems used in the two schools but also that certain "errors" in the writing of American business letters were not so regarded in London, or vice versa. Students in secretarial classes discovered anew the need to understand time zones as they learned about trans-Atlantic and world-wide telephone calls.

English, Speech and Drama. Reading lists in English classes were revised to include more titles relating to non-Western cultures, more travel books, and more recent biographies of modern world figures. As an outgrowth of a required course in public speaking, a Speakers Corps was organized to send teams of students to speak before service clubs and other community groups on topics related to current world affairs. The Asia Society provided many reading lists, as well as a collection of books for use in the high school. In a recent midyear examination in eleventh grade English a wide variety of topics (social, domestic, scientific and political) was provided in a composition question. In one section of twenty-eight students, nine students or one-third of the entire group chose to write on the topic, "Helping the People of Backward Countries." No other topic approached this one in popularity.

Foreign Languages. Apart from the introduction of elementary French and German in the junior high school, which was an ITWA innovation, a new interest in the life and culture of the peoples speaking those languages developed in the high school. Advertising posters for school events, and directions for use of the lunchroom often appeared in multi-language translations provided by ambitious students. A language laboratory was installed which changed radically the methods of language instruction.

Guidance. Increasingly the guidance counselors received requests for information about colleges having overseas study programs, about foreign service examinations, and about job opportunities in the field of international relations. Soon a committee of students under the sponsorship of a counselor began a systematic study of college catalogues and other sources to locate this type of information. Eventually their collection was incorporated in the guidance office library.

Health and Physical Education. A study of athletics on the world scene was initiated by the collection of information about the Olympic Games. Teachers and students alike were surprised to discover difficulties in locating reliable information on this subject. The effect of the Cold War on the Olympic Games gave new meaning to world affairs. Soon the teachers were questioning the philosophy and methods of physical education in other countries. A college specialist in physical education who had taken part in many international educational conferences was called in.

She helped the teachers of physical education to redefine their own aims and methods. As a result of this conference a new program and schedule for instruction in physical education was prepared for the Glens Falls Schools.

Hobbies and Leisure Time Activities. Mindful of the educational worth of many leisure time pursuits, stamp collecting, serious-purpose travel, and the entertainment of overseas visitors in the home were encouraged. The principal of the high school, a philatelist, wrote a paper for beginners, describing the first steps in and some of the pitfalls of stamp collecting. This paper was reproduced and distributed to elementary teachers. An increased number of visitors sponsored by the Experiment in International Living were invited to homes in the community.

Homemaking. Teachers of foods and clothing in the homemaking department found that students were interested in learning about food and clothing in other lands. One teacher prepared a successful unit on "Food Patterns and Customs of Other Countries." Repeated annually, the unit can be adapted to capitalize on the interest aroused by the visits of nationals from various countries. Students in these classes discovered new uses for maps, newspapers and periodicals in widening their horizons of meal planning and preparation.

Industrial Arts. In mechanical drawing, woodworking, automobile mechanics, and machine shop classes the world affairs approach resulted in the inclusion of many new topics. Drafting classes, for example, tried to cope with the great problem of map making, projecting a round globe on a flat sheet of paper. As a part of the woodworking course the sources of valuable lumber were investigated and the origin of many of the special finishes used in fine work were studied. In automobile mechanics, economics of world trade in foreign cars as well as the mechancial principles of European compact cars received attention. Machine shop classes compared the British system of measurements with the metric system, a system gaining increasing world acceptance.

Mathematics. Teachers of mathematics gave students an opportunity to compare a tenth grade examination used in a Soviet school with one of their own. Students discovered that mathematics is a constant requirement in the secondary schools of the

Soviet Union. These observations, together with the emphasis in the "new" mathematics in their own classes, have provided a new perspective on mathematics as an intellectual pursuit throughout the world.

Music. In addition to the aesthetics, and the history and cultural background of music of the Western nations, the ITWA program has called attention to national anthems of countries new and old. It has also focused attention on the differences and the similarities in the music of ethnic groups in all parts of the world. Recordings of Asian and African music have been added to the music department's collection. Teachers and students have become more sensitive to the international values and uses of music.

Science. The science program in the senior high school includes courses in biology, physics and chemistry. Because of the ITWA program an effort has been made to stress the international values of science and the gains made possible by international cooperation. The biology course has included special units on world diseases, the program of WHO, population growth, food supply, and the benefits of research. In the physics course the scientific principles of radio broadcasting have been taught in connection with problems of government regulations and social control of radio. The chemistry course has one unit on "Men of Science." This unit brings out the contributions to science of men from many lands and develops the point that science knows no national boundaries.

Social Studies. The social studies program has been changed to provide much greater emphasis on the non-Western world. All of the cultural areas are now receiving attention. The origin of the great revolutions of the 18th century—the democratic political revolution and the Industrial Revolution in Western Europe, and their gradual extension to other cultural regions provided a basis for understanding much that has happened in the world since that time. The courses in world history and American history had to be broadened and deepened to bring them into harmony with the ITWA program. To stimulate and to recognize accomplishment in the inter-disciplinary study of world affairs several prizes ("World Affairs Awards") are offered each year to members of the high school graduating class. These awards, totaling two hundred dollars, are given in the name of the Glens Falls Rotary Club. Applicants are advised to submit a brief description or listing of their achievements in more than one subject field or co-curricular activity. The supporting evidence in the form of notebooks, essays, newspaper clippings, program participation, exhibit materials, and correspondence is submitted in a portfolio. A committee of teachers representing all subject fields involved in the activities reported by the applicants makes the determination of the awards.

In addition to these curricular activities, high school students as individuals and as groups have become acquainted with many teen-age students from overseas. Delegates to the Herald Tribune High School Forum have been entertained in homes of students for two- and three-week periods and have attended the high school. A chapter of American Field Service has been organized to bring exchange students for one-year stays in the school and community. The Experiment in International Living has sent groups of students from time to time, including the vacation season. The Glens Falls Rotary Club has underwritten for one year the expenses of a student from Kenya studying at Glens Falls High School and the Adirondack Community College. These students, too, have enjoyed hospitality in the homes of high school students. Besides foreign students, a number of other overseas visitors, teachers for the most part, have come to Glens Falls for short-term visits under the auspices of such exchange programs as the Institute of International Education, the Governmental Affairs Institute, and the Office of Education. From our experience, one conclusion can be stated emphatically—meeting a person from another culture is a highly effective introduction to that culture. Since 1957, Glens Falls schools and community have entertained more than two hundred visitors from sixty nations.

The following activities were also part of the program, attempted by one or more teachers in *grades ten through twelve:*

1. Read regularly an English-language newspaper or magazine published in another country such as Canada, U. K., India, Pakistan, or Switzerland.
2. Make a diagram comparing the government of the U. S. with that of another country.

3. Prepare an exhibit to show how maps are used to report U.N. membership, population growth, democratic governments, alliances, illiteracy, etc.
4. Compare the views of a scientist and a statesman on such topics as disarmament, nuclear energy, population growth, public health, etc.
5. Compare the views of an English teacher, a history teacher, a science teacher, and one other on a given topic or set of data such as the need for radio regulation or rate of literacy in a given country.
6. Prepare a chart or graph to include: Western and non-Western countries, size of land area and population, and approximate time when industrial development began.
7. Read novels written in English about other lands.
8. Read, in translation, novels and poetry from other languages.
9. Make a list of the most popular games and sports in several countries.
10. Listen to recordings of indigenous music of several cultural areas.
11. Compare two or more newspaper accounts from different countries of the same important event.
12. Arrange to show prints or slides of art from various countries.
13. Make a general survey of countries to compare such information as: observance of Sabbath by the various religious groups, national heroes and national holidays, Nobel Prize winners in various fields, style and use of family and given names, status of women, etc.
14. Compile a list of commonly used stereotypes of nationalities and comment on their validity.
15. Share in the school effort to entertain overseas guests in homes, schools, and community life, including fund raising.
16. Visit the U. N. as a member of an organized student group.
17. Make a list of American authors to be recommended to overseas students.
18. Participate in competitions for prizes and awards based on achievement in world affairs understanding.
19. Recomend a new book on world affairs for purchase by the school library.

A Concluding Note About the Activities

The ITWA is an on-going and developing program in the Glens Falls public schools. Successful experiences and learning activities may or may not be repeated from one year to another. The heart of the program is not in a curriculum guide, nor a set of lesson plans, valuable as these are, but rather in a point of view. We believe that instruction in all grades and subjects can reflect, in one way or another, a world point of view. We believe that this emphasis is of crucial importance in the education of young Americans for life in the 20th century.

Appendix

Part I. Evaluation

WHAT did the ITWA program in Glens Falls accomplish?

Answers to this question will be found in either or both of two sources. They will be found in the responses of pupils, teachers, and townspeople. They will also be found in the results of the formal testing program. This chapter contains a summary of both types of evaluation. The Appendix to this report includes a sample of some of the evaluation instruments used in the formal testing program.

THE EVALUATION PROGRAM

The experimental evaluation program was limited to the classroom. Primarily because of lack of instruments, no systematic attempt was made to measure to what extent and in what way the three-year experiment influenced the teachers. Nor, due to lack of resources, was any formal effort made to determine what influence the program had upon the community as a whole. As a result of these two gaps in the evaluation program, all conclusions in regard to the influence of ITWA upon teachers and townspeople must rest upon the subjective evidence of personal testimony.

The formal evaluation was made with the assistance of staff members from the Educational Testing Service of Princeton, New Jersey. These included Dr. William Angoff, Assistant Director, Statistical Analysis Division; Miss Barbara Peace, Test Development Division; and Mr. Robert Solomon, Director, Test Development Division. Dr. Angoff analyzed the results of the evaluation and prepared the report which is summarized in the following paragraphs.

The plan for evaluating the ITWA program in Glens Falls involved testing a group of students in the fall of 1958, and the retesting at the termination of the program eighteen months later in the spring of 1960, when the students were enrolled in the following grade. Another school system in New York State was chosen as the "control" community, where normal and usual instruction in social studies would be carried out without the special emphasis on the study of world affairs. The community chosen was selected because of its similarity to Glens Falls in terms of size (population in 1950: 17,000-20,000) and in terms of socio-economic variables.

In order to provide a broader base for generalizing the results of the program, the evaluation study was carried out at three grade levels, grades 5-6, 8-9, and 11-12. Initial testing was done in the fall of 1958 in the first of each pair of grades; final testing of the same students was carried out at the second of each pair of grades eighteen months later, in the spring of 1960.

The plan for evaluating the program for "Improving the Teaching of World Affairs" was one that is generally considered by the specialists in the field of educational measurement to be most appropriate for methods experiments. In brief, the plan called for two determinations of student performance—one at the beginning of the administration of the program and the other at its termination—as well as the use of two groups of students—the experimental group, to whom the program of instruction was administered, and the control group, similar to the experimental group in all important respects except that it received conventional instruction. It is of some interest to point out that in this type of experiment, both the measurements and the groups are controlled. The pre-test measurement serves as a base line against which to evaluate the post-test measurement; the control group serves as a base line against which to evaluate the experimental group. In the absence of the controls provided by either the pre-test or by the control group only the most limited generalizations would be possible. Without the pre-test and the knowledge of initial status, for example, it would be impossible to know the specific effect of the period of time during which instruction took place. For example, it could be argued—and quite reasonably so—that the post-test scores earned by the higher-scoring of the groups were simply the result of the fact that they were a more able group, both at the time of the pre-test as well as at the time of the post-test; and that the particular program of instruction was immaterial to their score gains. Without the control group it could be argued —and just as reasonably—that the observed growth from pre- to post-testing would have resulted from even the most casual program of instruction, or simply from natural "growth," and that it is not necessarily uniquely attributable to the specific program of instruction that was actually carried out. It could be argued that any program, or no program at all, might have yielded a pre-test-post-test growth differential equal in magnitude to the one actually observed, or even greater.

The method of analysis employed throughout the course of the study was the method of covariance analysis. This method provides for the test of differences between the two groups in their post-test performance, *after* adjusting for any differences that might be present in their pre-test performance before the initiation of the program of instruction. The particular procedure followed is that described by Gulliksen and Wilks.[8] It should be pointed out that the method of covariance analysis rests on the assumption that the groups chosen for the experiment differ only randomly at the outset. In the ITWA experiment this was not, of course true, since the groups were taken intact from their own communities. However, it is believed that this departure from strict adherence to the theory of the statistical method did not seriously invalidate the results of the study.

There was, however, one consideration which does cast some question on the generality of the results of the present study. This has to do with the time of administration of the testing instruments. Ordinarily, in collecting data for a covariance analysis for an educational methods experiment, the control test is admin-

---

[8] H. Gulliksen and S. S. Wilks. "Regression Tests for Several Samples." *Psychometrika* 15:91-114; 1950.

istered before any exposure to the experimental conditions. As indicated previously, this administration provides the measurement that is taken as a base line for later comparisons. Such a procedure was not followed in the present study. The pre-tests were administered fully a year after the ITWA program was under way. Therefore, all comparisons, evaluations, and conclusions were made with that measurement as the base line. If there were differential effects for the two groups during the first year of the program—if, for example, the Glens Falls groups learned significantly more than the corresponding control groups during the first year—these effects would not be observed. The conclusions of the evaluation are therefore necessarily restricted to the changes that took place during the last two of the three years during which the program was in operation.

In the fall of 1958 the tests described below were administered to students in grades 5, 8, and 11 in Glens Falls and in the control school. These tests were again administered to the same students at the "formal" termination of the ITWA program in the spring of 1960.

a. *Cooperative Sequential Tests of Educational Progress (STEP) in Social Studies.* This test was designed through the joint effort of experienced social studies teachers and test experts to identify and measure the important outcomes of social studies instruction. The emphasis in this test is on the critical abilities and basic understandings which are primary goals of instruction in the social studies throughout the grades. The test is available in different forms, pitched at successive levels of ability. Alternate forms at the same level are also available. The scores are reported on a single derived-score scale so that inter- and intra-student and group comparisons can be made, irrespective of the particular forms and levels taken. In the present study students took the forms of the test appropriate to their level of education. In order to avoid recall of particular test items, student took different forms of the test in the initial and final testing sessions.

b. *An Achievement Test in World Affairs.* This test was especially constructed for the present evaluation. Three forms were prepared so that students at different levels could take different forms. Only one form, however, was available at each level.

c. *Information Inventory*. This test was intended to measure involvement in activities that might reflect an interest in foreign peoples and countries. It was prepared especially for the purpose of this evaluation and was made available in three forms, each appropriate for a different level of maturity.

d. *Attitude Survey*. This test was of the Likert type (Yes, No, Don't Know), calling for responses reflecting an enlightened and tolerant attitude toward members of various racial and national groups. Like the World Affairs Test and the Information Inventory, this test was prepared especially for the present evaluation and was made available in three forms, each for a different level of maturity.

We turn now to the results of the four tests. Because the STEP test was the only one in the battery which permitted comparisons between levels as well as with the published norms, the results of that test received major attention.

It is interesting to note that the pre-test, given in 1958, showed that students in both communities were superior, on the average, to students in the nation as a whole, with Glens Falls ranking higher than the control school system. A different form of the same test, given in 1960, revealed that students in both communities had made significant gains. Glens Falls students had significantly higher mean scores (beyond the five percent level) at grades 6, 9, and 12. It was also observed that the difference in scores between the two school systems increased at each level until grade 11, where it fell off slightly. At grade 12 it was observed that the difference in scores was so slightly in favor of Glens Falls as to cause the experimental school system to lose virtually all its former advantage over the control community.

The evaluation report was somewhat more reserved in its conclusions with regard to the World Affairs Test. This test was prepared by Glens Falls teachers in cooperation with test specialists from the Educational Testing Service. Generally speaking, the results of the World Affairs Test appeared to bear out the conclusions drawn from the STEP test results: (1) The Glens Falls students were superior to the control students at all grade levels, both before and after the experimental period. All score gains—in both communities and at all three levels—were significant gains. (2) In general, these results confirmed the findings already observed in connection with the STEP test. The score gains at Glens Falls were greater than those in the control school system at two levels—grades 5-6 and 8-9, but less at grades 11-12.

Both of these tests we have been discussing—the STEP Social Studies test and the World Affairs Test—were concerned with "cognitive knowledge and understanding." The other two tests—Information Inventory and Attitude Survey—attempted to measure the elusive qualities of interest and attitudes. Specifically, the Information Inventory (the title is misleading) undertook to measure *interest* in foreign peoples and countries; the Attitude Survey, as its title indicates, was designed to measure degree of tolerance toward people of various racial and national origins. According to the evaluation report, the results of both the tests were "obscure." Neither test revealed a consistent pattern of superiority for one community over the other, either before or after the period of instruction. The only significant gains occurred at grades 5-6.

The evaluation report suggested that quite possibly the ITWA program was more effective at the lower grade levels. Were that the case, then data emerging from the study of a program of this sort would give evidence of its effect in such an instrument as the Information Inventory, designed to measure involvement in activities related to interest in foreign peoples. From reports of the activities which are part of the ITWA program—reports which describe lectures, exhibits, visits, movies, all of them seemingly designed to evoke interest in the culture and customs of foreign peoples, rather than in the politics and economics of international affairs—one would expect this kind of interest, particularly in the younger students. It would be consistent with this hypothesis to speculate further that a program of this sort would not have a less marked effect on students at the higher grade levels. Among senior high school students attitudes and interest in leisure-time activities are undoubtedly more rigid and resistant to influences, perhaps particularly resistant to influences of the sort introduced by the ITWA program.

Continuing with its speculations, the evaluation report turned to a consideration of the "obscure" results of the Attitude Survey. It pointed out that whatever effects the ITWA program may have had on cognitive knowledge and understanding of social studies and world affairs and on the development of interest in foreign people, there may have been no change in attitudes of enlightened tolerance and permissiveness toward foreign people. This conclusion is difficult to accept, if it is granted that cognitive changes did take place. It is more likely that attitudinal changes did take place, but possibly of a subtle nature, beyond the sensitivity of the testing instrument. It is conceivable that the attitudinal changes, if they existed, took place only toward foreign people in their own setting, not toward foreign people in an American setting. It was toward attitudes of this latter type that the instrument was directed, while the instruction was directed to attitudes toward foreign people in foreign countries. Finally, it is possible that although the attitudes of these students were in the process of changing, these changes would not be noticed at once. Whereas the effects of cognitive learning take place immediately and are immediately noticeable, it takes longer to develop attitudinal "learning" of any permanent nature. On the other hand, the problem may be simply one of measurement, the report pointed out. The Attitude Survey used in the present evaluation may have lacked the degree of reliability, and what is probably more pertinent here, the degree of validity appropriate to the issue under consideration. For that reason it may not have been sufficiently sensitive to measure the kinds of attitudinal changes that may in fact have taken place.

Those concerned with evaluation were confronted with procedural problems as well as the basic inadequacy of the testing instruments. For one thing, the construction of the tests (with the exception of the standardized STEP test) could not begin until the experiment itself had started. As a result, the program had been going on a year before any tests were administered. Who can say that the experiment did not make its greatest impact during that first year? In the second place, the situation in regard to the "control" group left much to be desired. Ideally, the testing program should have been carried on in the control school without anyone in that school knowing the reasons for it. Unfortunately, this was not feasible. In order to secure cooperation of the control school for this time-consuming operation, reasons had to be given. But the moment the reasons were known, the control school became in a sense a "competitor." Once it was psychologically involved, that school system could no longer remain "neutral." The Hawthorne effect was inevitable.[9]

More serious than the procedural problems was the sheer inadequacy of the tests themselves. The art of testing has reached the point where gains in information can be measured with reasonable accuracy, and on this score the Glens Falls results were gratifying. But the measurement of interest and attitudes is something else again, and it is not surprising that in this aspect of the experiment the results were "obscure."

THE PARTICIPANTS SPEAK

Observers of the Glens Falls efforts to develop greater awareness of and sensitivity to the problems *and* the progress of the human family have been impressed with the thoughtful reactions this program has evoked among students, faculty, and laymen. The following paragraphs are representative of views freely expressed by people concerned with discovering *the most effective means* of building in the coming generation a vision of a better world and the will to play a part in translating that vision into reality.

At the end of the first year of ITWA, the Superintendent of the Glens Falls school system wrote to the Executive Secretary of the National Council for the Social Studies. "In any educational program," Superintendent Roberts observed, "there are three vital factors on which its degree of success depends—what is taught, how it is taught, and what motivation exists for learning. Without a desire to learn on the part of the recipient of the educational program, content and methodology are hollow shells. To ensure the success of any program, including the ITWA program now under way in our schools, it is imperative that all of these factors receive attention. In my opinion, this has happened in regard to

---

[9] The reference is to an effect observed in the Hawthorne plant of the Western Electric Company. In an experiment concerned with assembly line production methods, it appeared that employees who knew they were involved in an experiment continuously increased their piecework production regardless of whether working conditions were made more (or less) satisfactory.

ITWA during this school year . . . . It seems to me . . . that a good organization has been set up to communicate with teachers in classrooms as well as in faculty groups. There has been a recognition of the need for the re-orientation of teachers' viewpoints toward world affairs without attempting at the same time to dictate what that changed thinking should be. In other words, there has been a respect shown for subject matter and grade level interests . . . For these reasons, I believe we are in a sound position to continue into the second year the re-training of a staff, the refinement of a curriculum, and the search for better methods and materials for ITWA . . ."

The principal of the Junior High School wrote: "It is difficult to assess the importance of the ITWA project . . . . There are no instruments, no geiger counters to register the impact of the free flow of ideas or concepts or understandings that result from the teacher's purpose to make the subject of world understanding more meaningful to the pupils. However, a few things which I have observed firsthand suggest a new alertness resulting from the project. . . ."

A science teacher observed: "I can report, informally, that there are many evidences in facts taught and attitudes stressed as well as activities carried on which show attention to ITWA. The science syllabus lists such topics as the metric system (which was originated in France and is now being adopted in India); the principle of gravity (from the ancient world of Archimedes to the latest scientific exploration of the IGY); simple and complex machines (from the lever and the wheel to the self-starting automobile and jet propulsion airplanes of today). The names of many inventors (Trudeau, Grassi, Agassiz, Jenner, Edison, Koch, Marconi, Noguchi, Pasteur, De Forest, etc.) illustrate the international nature of scientific advances. Other concepts of importance include the interdependence of peoples (showing the world contributions to the making of an automobile or a telephone) and the problems to be solved, such as the need for water supply, or the disposal of atomic waste. Too, we have to watch for evidences of intolerance and inability to get along with others. How can we hope to improve world affairs unless a student can adjust to the boy or girl across the aisle?"

A high school student reported: "Through ITWA I have enjoyed many rewarding experiences. I was able to attend a conference at Pomfret, Connecticut, where the situation concerning the independence of the African countries south of the Sahara was discussed. Here two panel discussions were arranged—one composed of the mother countries of Europe and the other of the former colonies in Africa. People from each country participated, presenting their ideas. I have also had the opportunity to correspond with a girl from France (which helped me with my French!) and now I am preparing to write to a girl from Israel. Throughout our classes we learn about other countries. In our English class we made a study of books dealing with the ways of life in several countries. In speech classes we presented debates and discussions on world affairs. There is also a Speakers' Corps where students' debating teams present their 'pros and cons' involving world affairs to the organizations in Glens Falls. I especially like this, because it gives us a chance to express ourselves. Through this program, Improving the Teaching of World Affairs, I have had the opportunity to meet people from all over the world. My ideas have become broader through understanding and being able to witness their opinions and reactions to their countries and to mine."

A citizen of the community volunteered his endorsement: "As one who has spent his active life as a career officer of the American Foreign Service, I was naturally interested when I learned that our Glens Falls school system was embarking on a program for improving the teaching of world affairs. There is no doubt whatever in my mind that the generation of Americans now in school, and those to follow, are going to have to have a different outlook on the world than did ours, or our fathers'. Like it or not, our country shares the globe with a lot of other nations which have as much right to be here as we have; and if there is to be any hope of peace between us, there must be a greater degree of cooperation than there has been. Cooperation starts with understanding.

"I am not talking 'internationalism' in the derogatory sense in which the word is sometimes used, meaning the reverse of patriotism. And I have little faith in special courses that purport to teach internationalism. It seems to me that the program now under way here, of awakening student interest in and awareness of other peoples and their problems and aspirations—as a by-product, one might say, of their regular studies—is a far better way to prepare our youth for intelligent citizenship than the self-glorification of the professional patriot or the appeasing approach of those who equate patriotism with chauvinism.

"It is particularly gratifying to me, as a citizen of Glens Falls, that our schools have embarked on such a program. I believe it is sober truth, not merely an expression of civic pride, to say that ours is fertile soil for the seeds of international understanding and cooperation for the mutual benefit of ourselves and our neighbors. Witness our continuing support of the Community Ambassador Project, the exchange of students and teachers who are welcomed to our schools, and the foreign doctors who regularly intern at our local hospital. If the program for improving the teaching of world affairs has merit, as I firmly believe it has, I know of no better place to put it to the test. But don't expect miracles. If the program is to produce visible results, it must be a continuing one."

Not one of the persons we have just quoted—Superintendent, principal, teachers, student, community leader—spoke with publication in mind. Each had something to say, and he said it. The important consideration is that they all believed that the effort to improve the teaching of world affairs was good—good for them as individuals, good for the schools and the community, good for the country, and good for the world.

Today, six years after the experiment started and three years after the pilot study as such came to an end, the Glens Falls story is continuing. It is a story that deserves telling and emulation in other communities in the United States and in other lands.

Part II. Evaluation Instruments

Many of the conclusions about the Glens Falls program are not based on results obtained from the use of paper and pencil tests and inventories. From necessity, evaluation must be conceived on a broader basis than testing. Knowing that teachers may be interested in the written evaluation instruments used in the Glens Falls Project, we are reproducing parts of three tests:

1. Achievement Test in World Affairs: Level A (Grades 10-12), Level B (Grades 7-9), Level C (Grades 4-6).
2. Attitude Survey: Level A, Level B, Level C.
3. Information Inventory: Level A, Level B, Level C.

ACHIEVEMENT TEST IN WORLD AFFAIRS: LEVEL A (GRADES 10-12)

Directions: Inside of this test book you will find some questions about people, places, and things in the world today. Each question is followed by five suggested answers. Choose the answer you think is best by drawing a circle around the letter in front of it.

1. Which of these countries has had the greatest cultural influence on the countries of Latin America?
   - (A) Italy
   - (B) France
   - (C) Spain
   - (D) Great Britain
   - (E) The United States

2. Which of the following is the chief reason why some people in the world have few of the comforts and conveniences most Americans have?
   - (A) They do not yet understand why democracy is superior to communism.
   - (B) They have not yet learned how to develop their resources and industries.
   - (C) They are not as intelligent as most Americans who have comforts and conveniences.
   - (D) They do not want to improve their ways of living.
   - (E) They have little desire to buy the things most Americans have.

3. Which of these statements about the United States' supply of natural resources is true?
   - (A) The United States is the only country in the world that has all it needs of every kind of natural resource.
   - (B) The United States has a large supply of natural resources but it still needs some things from other countries.
   - (C) The United States has few natural resources but its factories are able to produce everything the people need.
   - (D) The United States is very rich in a few natural resources but it is rather poor in most.
   - (E) The United States is rich in agricultural resources but it is rather poor in minerals.

4. Which of these is LEAST important as a reason why small foreign cars are becoming more and more popular in the United States?
   (A) They are cheaper to run than most American cars.
   (B) They can go faster than most American cars.
   (C) They are easier to park than most American cars.
   (D) They get more miles per gallon of gas than most American cars.
   (E) They are easier to handle in traffic than most American cars.

5. A person is said to be tolerant when he
   (A) does not believe in God
   (B) thinks that people do not have to obey laws which are injurious to them
   (C) believes that religion is more important than race
   (D) does not care what kind of government we have
   (E) thinks that everyone has a right to his opinion

6. The argument generally used by those who urge the United States government to limit the importation of European goods is that
   (A) European nations should pay for all their imports
   (B) European goods are unsuitable for the United States market
   (C) United States producers should be protected
   (D) Europe should be kept economically weak
   (E) United States consumers should be assured of lower prices

7. Which of the following would you NOT expect to find the United Nations Security Council discussing?
   (A) The labor problems of a member country
   (B) Problems concerned with international trade
   (C) A territorial dispute between two member countries
   (D) A naval war between a member country and a non-member country
   (E) The problems of member countries in trying to collect war debts

ACHIEVEMENT TEST IN WORLD AFFAIRS: LEVEL B (GRADES 7-9)

Directions: On this sheet you will find a number of questions. Each question is followed by five suggested answers. Choose the answer you think is best by drawing a circle around the letter in front of it.

1. Where does almost half of the world's population live?
   (A) Northwestern Europe
   (B) Northeastern United States
   (C) Southern and Eastern Asia
   (D) The Western Hemisphere
   (E) Russia

2. In which of these countries of the Eastern Hemisphere do the people have ways of living most like those of Western Europeans or Americans?
(A) India
(B) China
(C) Indonesia
(D) Korea
(E) Australia

3. The Charter of the United Nations is most like which of these?
(A) A law
(B) A court decision
(C) A constitution
(D) A deed
(E) An amendment

4. Which of these countries has the largest land area?
(A) Canada
(B) The United States
(C) China
(D) The Soviet Union
(E) India

5. Which of these statements about farmers all over the world is *false*?
(A) Some farmers in the world have never seen a tractor.
(B) Some farmers in the world grow only one crop.
(C) Some farmers in the world are very poor.
(D) Some farmers in the world cannot grow anything without irrigating their land.
(E) Some farmers in the world do not care what the weather is like.

6. A country is *neutral* when it
(A) does not takes sides in a war
(B) tries to bring about a settlement of a dispute between two countries
(C) agrees to take up arms against aggressors
(D) tries to annex territory
(E) is against war as a way of settling disputes

ACHIEVEMENT TEST IN WORLD AFFAIRS: LEVEL C (GRADES 4-6)

Directions: Here are some questions for you. After each question there are five suggested answers. Draw a circle around the letter in front of the answer you think is right.

1. Which of these countries has given us the most ideas for our laws and customs?
   (A) Spain
   (B) England
   (C) France
   (D) Germany
   (E) Italy

2. Which of these countries is most like the United States in climate and agriculture?
   (A) Argentina
   (B) Brazil
   (C) Columbia
   (D) Panama
   (E) Mexico

3. If you could visit all of these countries, which of these would you NOT expect to see?
   (A) A coconut grove in Switzerland
   (B) A herd of sheep in Australia
   (C) A fishing boat in Norway
   (D) A flower garden in the Netherlands
   (E) A rubber plantation in Malaya

4. In which of these countries do the citizens have the most to say about their government?
   (A) China
   (B) Egypt
   (C) Sweden
   (D) Spain
   (E) Poland

5. Which of these storybook people did we get from another country?
   (A) Paul Bunyan
   (B) Robin Hood
   (C) Davey Crockett
   (D) Rip Van Winkle
   (E) Uncle Remus

ATTITUDE SURVEY: LEVEL A (GRADES 10-12)

Directions: Below is a description of a boy who is about the same age as you are. Read the description and then answer the questions that follow.

Weng Chang was born in East Asia and came to the United States with his mother, father, and younger sister a few months ago. He has short, black hair and dark, slanting eyes, and he is not quite as tall as most American boys his age. He spends most of his time helping around the house and playing with his sister. Sometimes he watches the boys who live on the same street playing games, or fooling around with cars, or just talking. He'd like to join them, but he doesn't understand what they are doing. He is beginning to learn English but doesn't speak it very well.

Weng's father worked on a farm when the family first came to this country. He has just taken a job in a factory. In the old country, Mr. Chang was a leader in the village where the family lived. He doesn't have very much formal education, but he has taught himself a lot by reading on his own.

Mrs. Chang is a very small and very quiet woman. She takes care of the family's small apartment and the washing, mending, and cooking. She doesn't know very much about American food.

Answer the questions which follow "yes," "no," or "don't know" on the basis of what you have read about Weng Chang and of your understanding of people. On the line in front of each question, write Y if the answer is yes, N if the answer is no, or D if you don't know the answer.

_____ 1. Would you like to have the Changs live in your city?

_____ 2. Would you like to have Weng in your class in school?

_____ 3. Would you like to have Weng sit next to you in one of your classes?

_____ 4. Do you think your friends would mind if Weng joined you for lunch?

_____ 5. Do you think you could help Weng with his homework if he asked you for help?

_____ 6. Do you think your mother would want to help Weng's mother with her grocery shopping if you explained the situation to her?

_____ 7. Do you think Weng would ever make a varsity sports team?

_____ 8. Would you like to try to talk to Weng and help him with his English?

_____ 9. Do you think Weng would get mad if you couldn't understand what he was trying to say?

_____10. Would you like to visit Weng's home?

_____11. Do you think your parents would mind if Weng were invited to a party you were attending?

_____12. Do you think Weng might be a poor sport if he were on a losing team?

_____13. If he did something wrong, do you think Weng would tell the truth if the teacher asked him about it?

_____14. Do you think Weng might laugh at you if you made a mistake in class?

_____15. Do you think your teachers should give Weng special help with his English?

_____16. Would you like to listen to Weng tell the class about life in the old country?

_____17. Do you think Weng would make a good friend?

_____18. Do you think Weng might expect too much help from his teachers in keeping up with his school work?

_____19. Do you think Weng would be happier if he went to a special school for foreign-born students?

_____20. Do you think Weng would be kind to an older person?

_____21. Do you think Weng would be the kind to get into a lot of fights at school?

_____22. Do you think Weng's mother and father are good to him?

_____23. If Weng gets good marks in school, do you think he should be allowed to go on to college if he wants to?

_____24. Do you think that Weng could grow up to be a doctor or lawyer if he is smart enough?

_____25. Would you like to learn more about the country Weng came from?

_____26. Do you think Weng might be inclined to talk and laugh too loudly?

_____27. Do you think Weng's father could ever become a foreman in the factory where he works?

_____28. Do you think Weng would apologize if he ran into you in the hall and made you drop your books?

_____29. Would you mind it if Weng asked your sister or your friend's sister for a date?

_____30. Do you think Weng should ask American girls for dates?

Attitude Survey: Level B (Grades 7-9)

Directions: Below is description of a girl about your age. Read the description and then answer the questions which follow it.

Anna Kapinski, a dark-haired, dark-eyed girl, was born in Eastern Europe. She and her mother, father, and younger brother have just come to live in the United States. Anna is very thin and doesn't smile very often. She spends her time helping her mother take care of their small apartment and her little brother. When she sees girls her age outside laughing and talking, she would like to talk with them too, but she is just learning to speak English. Anna's clothes are different from the clothes the other girls wear.

Anna's father was a miner before coming to this country. Now he works on a large farm outside of town. He likes to work outdoors. Mrs. Kapinski is thin and dark like Anna. She gets up very early in the morning to pack her husband's lunch and get him off to work. She would like to take in washing and ironing in order to earn a little extra money, but it is hard for her to ask people for work because she can't talk to them very well.

Answer these questions about Anna by writing Y for "yes," N for "no," or D for "don't know."

_____ 1. Would you like to have the Kapinskis move to your city?

_____ 2. Do you think the Kapinskis will be as happy in America as they were in Europe?

_____ 3. Do you think Anna would enjoy being in your class in school?

_____ 4. Do you think your teacher would ask you to share a book with Anna if there weren't enough to go around?

_____ 5. Would you mind if Anna walked beside you in line?

_____ 6. If Anna came to your school and didn't talk to anybody, do you think your classmates should talk to her?

_____ 7. Do you know any people who would like to have Anna's mother do their washing and ironing?

_____ 8. Would you like to have Anna come to your house for supper?

_____ 9. Do you think Anna should feel funny about her clothes?

_____ 10. After she has learned English better, would you like to listen to Anna give a talk about what she thinks of life in America?

_____ 11. Do you think Anna would be so quiet it would not be fun to be with her?

_____ 12. Do you think Anna would lend you a pencil if you needed one?

_____ 13. Do you think Anna would be smart in school?

_____ 14. Do you think Anna will grow up to be a pretty girl?

_____ 15. Do you think Anna would enjoy reading a book in the library more than talking to you and your friends?

_____ 16. Do you think your friends would like Anna?

_____ 17. Do you think Anna's mother and father are proud of her?

_____ 18. Do you think Anna would do what the teacher tells her to do?

_____ 19. Do you think Anna might try to copy from someone's test paper if she could see it?

___20. Do you think Anna would tell the teacher if she saw someone looking at her test paper?

___21. If Anna found a dollar on the ground outside of school, do you think she would tell anyone about it?

___22. If she is smart enough, do you think Anna could grow up to be a nurse if she wanted to?

___23. If Anna came to your school, do you think your parents would be interested in hearing you talk about what she is like?

___24. Do you think Anna would be away from school a lot because of sickness?

___25. Do you think Anna will marry an American boy when she grows up?

___26. Do you think Anna would be happier if she went to a special school for slow-learning children?

___27. Do you think Anna might wear clothes to school that weren't as clean as they should be?

___28. Do you think your mother would want to help Anna's mother find work if you told her about it?

___29. Do you think your parents or neighbors would mind if the Kapinskis moved in next door to you?

___30. Do you think Anna could ever be elected to an office in your class?

ATTITUDE SURVEY: LEVEL C (GRADES 4-6)

Directions: Here are some questions that are about you.

1. Do you like to read stories about people like the Changs and the Kapinskis? Put an X in the line in front of the sentence that best tells how you feel about reading stories like these.

   _____ I don't mind reading stories about people like these but I like other kinds of stories a lot better.

   _____ I think that stories about people more like those I know are a lot more fun to read.

   _____ I don't like stories about people like these very much but I read them when I have to.

   _____ I think it's fun to read about people like these because they're so different from the people I know.

   _____ I wish I could read more stories about people like these and learn more about them.

2. Have you ever known anyone who was born in another country and came to the United States to live? _____ Yes _____ No
   If you have, what country did the person come from? _____
   _____

3. Have you ever known anyone who lived in another country for a long time and then came back to the United States? _____ Yes _____ No
   If you have, what country did the person live in? _____

4. Do you or does anyone in your family know how to speak any language besides English? _____ Yes _____ No
   If so, what language? _____

5. Have you ever been outside of the United States? _____Yes_____No
   If you have, what country or countries did you visit?
   Canada? _____   Mexico? _____   (Yes or No)
   Some other country? If so, write its name here: _____

6. If you and your family had the chance to visit any country in the world that you wanted to for a month, and it wouldn't cost anything, what country would you choose? _____
   Why would you like to visit this country? _____

   _____

   _____

   _____

   _____

INFORMATION INVENTORY: LEVEL A (GRADES 10-12)

Directions: This inventory contains some questions about your activities and your likes and dislikes. There are no "right" or "wrong" answers to these questions and your answers will not affect your school marks in any way. You should give answers that reflect what you really do and how you really feel. Answer the questions as accurately as you can.

1. On the lines below write the names of any newspapers or magazines that you enjoy reading. Then mark an X in the column that best describes how often you read each newspaper and magazine. (If you cannot remember the name of a particular paper or magazine, you may just put "newspaper" or "magazine" for that one and check the appropriate column.)

Name	How often read			
Newspapers	Almost Every Day	Three or Four Times a Week	Once a Week	Once in a While
_____	_____	_____	_____	_____
_____	_____	_____	_____	_____
_____	_____	_____	_____	_____
_____	_____	_____	_____	_____

Name _____   *How often read*

Magazines	Weekly	Monthly	Every Few Months	Two or Three Times a Year

2. Below are listed some things that are usually found in newspapers. On the line provided, number these things from 1 to 5 to show which you like best and which you like least. Put "1" in front of the part of the paper you like *best*, "2" in front of the part you like *second best*, and so on.

  _____ Comic strips
  _____ Stories about sports
  _____ Stories about weddings, parties, club activities
  _____ Stories about national and international happenings
  _____ Stories about movies, television, radio

3. Below are listed some things that are often found in magazines. Number these items in the same way as you did those in question 2.

  _____ Fiction stories
  _____ Stories about ordinary people who have done interesting things
  _____ Articles about travel
  _____ "How-to-do-it" articles
  _____ "Behind the scenes" articles about important news events

4. Are you now reading a book for pleasure, or have you finished one recently? If so, what is the author and title?

  _____

  If not, what was the name of the last book you remember reading for pleasure? _____

  How long ago did you read it? _____

5. If you had to make a book report for school and could pick a book on any topic you wanted, what topic would you most likely choose?

  _____

6. About how many times have you been to the public library in the last year?

  1-5 times ____; 5-10 times ____; 10-20 times ____; More than 20 times ____

7. Are there any particular programs that you look forward to on TV?
If so, please name two or three of these programs.

_____   _____
_____   _____
_____   _____
_____   _____

INFORMATION INVENTORY: LEVEL B (GRADES 7-9)

Directions:

1. Please list below any organizations, clubs, youth groups to which
you belong and in whose activities you take part *regularly*.

School clubs and organizations: *Church groups and organizations:*

_____   _____
_____   _____
_____   _____
_____   _____

Community organizations: *Other organizations:*
(Boy Scouts, Girl Scouts, Red Cross)

_____   _____
_____   _____
_____   _____
_____   _____

2. If you had the money, time, and ability to become anything you
wanted, what would you like most to be?

_____
_____
_____
_____

Directions: The statements below describe activities that some high
school students have been found to enjoy. If you had the chance you
might enjoy doing some of these things too. Read each statement and
decide whether or not you would like to do what it says. Then, on the
line in front of the number of each statement, write:

    Y for "yes" if you *would* like to do it,
    N for "no" if you *would not* like to do it,
    U for "uncertain" if you think you *might* like to do it, but you
    are not sure.

Would you like to

———— 1. Listen to a comedy program on the radio.
———— 2. Collect the autographs of famous people in sports or the movies.
———— 3. Make a poster showing pictures of interesting places in the world.
———— 4. Watch a TV program about life in another country.
———— 5. Visit a zoo or aquarium.
———— 6. Collect pictures of important people in the governments of various countries in the world.
———— 7. Watch a TV program about the life in the "Wild West."
———— 8. Learn how to say some words and phrases in a foreign language.
———— 9. Go on a camping trip with your friends or family.
————10. Tour the United Nations building in New York.
————11. Watch a movie short about the social customs followed in different countries.
————12. Help the school librarian catalog some new books.
————13. Go to a party or dance with a group of friends.
————14. Read a story about the adventures of an explorer in the far North.
————15. Write a story about a heroic animal.
————16. Write letters to someone your age in another country.
————17. Show a foreign visitor around your school.
————18. Listen to a sports broadcast on the radio.
————19. Watch a parade.
————20. Draw pictures of people you know or things you have seen.

INFORMATION INVENTORY: LEVEL C (GRADES 4-6)

Directions: On these pages there are some questions about things you do or would like to do. There are no "right" or "wrong" answers to these questions. You should answer them by putting down what you really do or how you really feel. Your answers will not affect your school marks in any way. Answer the questions as carefully as you can.

1. Below are some different kinds of stories. On the line in front of each kind of story, put a number from 1 to 5 to show how much you like that kind of story. Put "1" in front of the kind you like *best,* "2" in front of the kind you like *next best,* and "3," "4," or "5" in front of the others to show how well you like them. ("5" will be in front of the kind you like *least.*)

———— Stories about people in faraway places
———— Stories about animals

_____ Fairy tales and stories about make-believe people and things

_____ Stories about real things that happened a long time ago

_____ Stories about things that are happening in the world today

2. Do you like to look at newspapers? _____ Yes _____ No

If you do, put an X on one of these lines to show about how often you look at a newspaper:

_____ Almost every day

_____ About once a week

_____ Once in a while

_____ I hardy ever look at one

3. Do you like to read magazines? _____ Yes _____ No

If you do, on the lines below write the names of some of the magazines you like best. Then mark X in the column which best tells about your reading.

Names of Magazines	I read it every week	I read it every month	I read it once in a while	I hardly ever read it

4. Are you now reading a book (not a school book), or have you just finished one? _____ Yes _____ No

If so, what is the name of it? _____

If not, what is the name of the last book you remember reading?

_____

5. If you had to read a book for school and could pick any kind of book you wanted, what kind would you choose?

I would choose a book about _____

6. Are there any special programs that you like to watch on TV? Write down the names of two or three of the programs you like best.

_____

_____

7. You may be a member of some of the clubs or groups on this list. Put an X in front of any that you belong to.

＿＿＿ Cub Scouts
＿＿＿ Brownies
＿＿＿ Church Club
＿＿＿ Junior Red Cross

Do you belong to any school clubs? ＿＿＿ Yes ＿＿＿ No
If so, please write their names on these lines.

＿＿＿＿＿＿＿＿＿＿＿＿＿＿   ＿＿＿＿＿＿＿＿＿＿＿＿＿＿

＿＿＿＿＿＿＿＿＿＿＿＿＿＿   ＿＿＿＿＿＿＿＿＿＿＿＿＿＿

Do you belong to any other clubs or groups? ＿＿＿ Yes ＿＿＿ No
If so, write their names on these lines.

＿＿＿＿＿＿＿＿＿＿＿＿＿＿   ＿＿＿＿＿＿＿＿＿＿＿＿＿＿

＿＿＿＿＿＿＿＿＿＿＿＿＿＿   ＿＿＿＿＿＿＿＿＿＿＿＿＿＿

Part III. Aids to Teachers

Teaching, like learning, thrives on motivation. Motivation is gained and accelerated by various experiences. The experiences which help a teacher to develop a world affairs point of view are of several sorts: personal travel, entertainment of overseas visitors, personal interest in an overseas assignment of a family member or a friend, formal study, mass media offerings, or a systematic reading.

Once a teacher has gained a world point of view, by whatever means, he becomes concerned to learn more about what the people of the world think, feel and do. He will become more concerned about his own country and its role in world affairs. Sustained reading will help him to widen and deepen his insights. At the outset he will be impressed, not by the lack, but by the plethora of materials related to world affairs.

The following annotated list of selected readings, gleaned from a much larger collection of materials assembled that proved especially helpful in Glens Falls, are cited as examples of materials that should be helpful to teachers in beginning a collection of readings for his own or his students' use.

SELECTED BIBLIOGRAPHY
Books and Pamphlets

1. Anderson, Howard R., Editor, *Apporaches to an Understanding of World Affairs.* Twenty-Fifth Yearbook of the National Council for the Social Studies, 1201 Sixteenth Street, N.W., Washington, D.C. 20036, 1954, cloth bound, 478 pp., $4.00.

   A scholarly introduction to the problems of world tensions and ways of living in several regions, together with suggestions for teaching, at all levels, an understanding of world affairs.

2. Brockington, Fraser, *World Health.* A Pelican Book A-425, paper bound, 405 pp., 95¢.

   A penetrating analysis of the prospects and problems of everyman's chief concern—his health, treated from an international viewpoint with especial reference to the work of the World Health Organization.

3. Cole, J. P., *Geography of World Affairs.* Penguin Books, Inc., Baltimore 11, Maryland, A Penguin Special, A-548, 1963, paper bound, 319 pp., $1.25.

   A Western treatment of the world by regions, dealing with physical and human geography and identifying facts and issues of present world tensions.

4. Commager, Henry Steele, Editor, *Contemporary Civilization.* Scott, Foresman & Co., 433 E. Erie St., Chicago 11, Ill., 1959, paper bound, #1, 207 pp.; 1961, #2, 269 pp.; 1964, #3, 288 pp.

   Three symposiums of original essays on regional aspects of world affairs by recognized scholars. The essays are grouped for topical use in high school classes.

5. Dean, Vera Micheles, *The Nature of the Non-Western World.* The New American Library of World Literature, 501 Madison Avenue, New York 22, N.Y., A Mentor Book MD0190, 1957, paper bound, 288 pp., 60¢.

   A provocative discussion of the two major, modern revolutions—the industrial and the democratic—which, together with other factors of Western civilization, are stirring the rest of mankind to new hopes and ambitions.

6. Goetz, Delia, *World Understanding Begins With Children.* Bulletin 1949 No. 17, Reprinted 1955, United States Department of Health, Education, and Welfare, Office of Education, Washington 25, D.C., 30 pp., 20¢.

A practical, short explanation to aid the elementary teacher, especially in finding ways to teach about world affairs.

7. Kenworthy, Leonard S., *Free and Inexpensive Materials on World Affairs.* Bureau of Publications, Teachers College, Columbia University, New York, N.Y., 1963, $1.00.

This booklet supplies an excellent list of addresses from which to obtain materials about world affairs, U.S. foreign policy, regions and individual countries, and the United Nations and its specialized agencies and commissions.

8. ————, *Introducing Children to the World; in Elementary and Junior High Schools.* Harper & Brothers, Publishers, New York, 1956, 268 pp., $3.75.

A useful handbook to help teachers in planning how to teach international understanding.

9. ————, *Telling the UN Story—New Approaches to Teaching About the United Nations and Its Related Agencies.* Oceana Publications, Inc., Dobbs Ferry, N.Y., 166 pp., $2.00.

Written for UNESCO, this book contains a wealth of practical suggestions and is a valuable aid to teachers who seek to meet their responsibilities in the field of international understanding.

10. *North Central Association of Colleges and Secondary Schools, Foreign Relations Project. Foreign Relations Series.* Laidlaw Brothers, River Forest, Illinois. Price 80¢ each (A Teachers' Guide accompanies each booklet in the Series; Teachers' Guides 25¢ each.)

> *Africa and the World Today* by Rosberg
> *America's Role in the Middle East* by Jones
> *America's Stake in Western Europe* by Deutsch
> *Chinese Dilemma* by Armstrong
> *India and the World Today* by Kublin
> *The United States and the Soviet Challenge* by Platig
> *The United States and World Affairs* by Platig
> *Southeast Asia and American Policy* by Armstrong
> *The United States in the United Nations* by Nolde
> *The United States' Role in Latin America* by Blanksten

11. *Other Lands, Other Peoples. A Country-by-Country Fact Book.* Committee on International Relations, National Education Association, Third Edition, 1964, $1.50 litho.

A ready-reference book, in lithograph, which provides brief, up-to-date information especially useful when overseas visitors are entertained.

12. *Resources for Teaching About the United Nations.* With annotated bibliography; Committee on International Relations of the National Education Association, 1962, $1.50.

13. *Scholastic World Affairs.* Multi-texts; Kenneth M. Gould, Editorial Director, Scholastic Book Services, 33 West 42nd Street, New York 36, N.Y., 65¢ each.

> *The Subcontinent of India*
> *The Two Chinas*
> *Emerging Africa*
> *The Soviet Union*
> *The Soviet Satellites*
> *The Rim of Asia*

14. *Scott, Foresman Series on Area Studies in Economic Progress.* Scott, Foresman and Company, Chicago, Ill., 1963. Package price (5 booklets), $4.80; Specimen set (1 copy of each booklet and 1 Guidebook), $6.72.

> *India—Struggle Against Time* by Berkowitz
> *Japan—Lessons in Enterprise* by Hunsberger
> *Latin America—Reform or Revolution* by Madden
> *The Middle East—Old Problems and New Hopes* by Babian
> *The Soviet Union—Communist Economic Power* by Schwartz
> *sub-Saharan Africa—Struggle Against the Past* by Salkever and
>   Flynn
> *Western Europe and the Common Market* by Calderwood

15. *Worldmark Encyclopedia of the Nations.* Editor and Publisher, Moshe Y. Sachs, Edited by Louis Barron, Worldmark Press, Inc., Harper & Row, Publishers, New York, N.Y., a library reference work in five volumes.

A practical guide to the geographic, historical, political, social, and economic status of all nations, their international relationships, and the United Nations system.

Periodicals

1. *Africa Report,* The African-American Institute, Inc., Suite 505, Dupont Circle Bldg., Washington 6, D.C.

2. American Education Press, American Education Publications, Wesleyan University Press, Inc., Education Center, Columbus, Ohio.

> *Current Events*
> *Every Week*
> *Our Times*

3. *American Universities Field Staff Reports,* American Universities Field Staff, 366 Madison Avenue, New York 17, N.Y.

4. Civic Education Service, 1733 K Street, N.W., Washington 6, D.C.

> *The American Observer*
> *The Weekly News Review*
> *The Junior Review*
> *The Young Citizen*
> *Headline-Focus Wall Map*

5. *Focus,* American Geographical Society, Broadway at 156th Street, New York 32, N.Y.

6. *Foreign Policy Briefs*, ($1.00 per year) and *The Department of State Bulletin*, ($8.50 per year). United States Department of State, Washington, D.C. 20520.

7. *Great Decisions*, Foreign Policy Association, Inc., 345 East 46th Street, New York 17, N.Y.

8. *The Hindu Weekly Review*, The Hindu, 40 East 49th Street, New York 17, N.Y.

9. *Intercom, A World Affairs Handbook*, An instrument for the exchange of information about what people are doing to learn, teach, consider or influence what is going on in the world. See especially Vol. 5, No. 5, October 1963, $1.00, "Teaching World Affairs—A Special Guide for Educators and Program Planners," which covers general materials, bibliographies, arms control and disarmament, United Nations, world trade and economic development, teaching about Communism, Asia, Europe, Latin America, Middle East and the Soviet Union. It lists a series of periodicals and pamphlets, resource materials, selected audio-visual sources, etc.

10. *Manchester Guardian*, Manchester Guardian, 20 East 53rd Street, New York 22, N.Y.

11. *Panorama*, World Confederation of Organizations of the Teaching Profession, 1227 16th Street, N.W. Washington 6, D. C.

12. Scholastic Magazines, 902 Sylvan Avenue, Englewood Cliffs, New Jersey.

    News Pilot (Grade 1)
    News Ranger (Grade 2)
    News Trails (Grade 3)
    News Explorer (Grade 4)
    Newstime (Grades 5, 6)
    Junior Scholastic (Grades 6-8)
    World Week (Grades 8-10)
    Senior Scholastic (Grades 10-12)

13. *Unesco Courier*, UNESCO Publications Center, 801 Third Avenue, New York 22, N.Y.

14. Weekly news magazines such as: *Time, Newsweek, U.S. News and World Report*.

15. *World Affairs Study Guide*, Mrs. Ruth G. Shipley, World Affairs Program, Minneapolis Star, Minneapolis 15, Minn.

WHERE TO WRITE FOR FREE MATERIALS, PUBLICATIONS LISTS, SPEAKERS, AND OTHER INFORMATION

American Association for the United Nations (AAUN), 345 East 46th Street, New York 17, N.Y.

Conference Group of the U.S. National Organizations on the United Nations, 331 38th Street, New York 16, N.Y.

American Library Association, 50 East Huron Street, Chicago 11, Ill.

Food and Agriculture Organization of the United Nations, United Nations, New York 17, N.Y.

Freedom from Hunger Foundation, 700 Jackson Place, N.W., Washington 6, D.C.

U.S. Committee for the United Nations, 375 Park Avenue, New York 22, N.Y.

U.S. Committee for UNICEF, United Nations Children's Fund, United Nations, New York 17, N.Y.

U.S. Committee for Palestine Refugees (UNRWA), United Nations, New York 17, N.Y. (Arab refugees from Israel)

U.S. National Commission for UNESCO, Department of State, Washington 25, D.C.

U.S. Mission to the United Nations, 799 United Nations Plaza, New York 17, N.Y.

United States Committee for Refugees, 20 West 40th Street, New York 18, N.Y.

United States Information Center, 1028 Connecticut Avenue, N.W., Washington 6, D.C.

United Nations Publishing Services, United Nations, New York 17, N.Y. (To inquire about books in print.)

United Nations Educational, Scientific, and Cultural Organization (UNESCO), United Nations, New York 17, N.Y.

National Council for Community Services for International Visitors, Meridian House, 1630 Crescent Place, N.W., Washington 9, D.C.

National Catholic Education Association, 1785 Massachusetts Avenue, N.W., Washington 6, D.C.

People to People Program, 2401 Grand Avenue, Kansas City 8, Mo.

Pan American Union, Constitution Avenue, N.W., Washington, D.C.

Pan American Health Organization, 1501 New Hampshire Avenue, N.W., Washington, D.C.

United States Department of State, Office of Media Services, Washington, D.C. 20520 (for various publications, film lists and posters).

World Health Organization (WHO), United Nations, New York 17, N.Y.

U.S. Office of Education, Division of International Education, Department of Health, Education, and Welfare, Washington 25, D.C.

Institute for International Order, 11 West 42nd Street, New York 17, N.Y.

World Confederation of Organizations of the Teaching Profession (WCOTP), 1227 Sixteenth Street, N.W., Washington 6, D.C.

American Council on Education, 1785 Massachusetts Avenue, N.W., Washington 6, D.C.

Institute for International Education, 800 2nd Avenue, New York 17, N.Y.

International Visitors Information Service, 700 Jackson Place, N.W., Washington, D.C.

World Rule of Law Center, Duke University, Durham, N.C.

United Nations Films: William M. Dennis Film Libraries, 2506½ West 7th Street, Los Angeles, Calif.; International Organization Affairs, State Department, Washington 25, D.C.; Contemporary Films, Inc., 267 West 25th Street, New York 1, N.Y.; or Contemporary Films, Inc., 614 Davis Street, Evanston, Ill.

Speaker Services for the United Nations, 345 East 46th Street, New York 17, N.Y.

Foreign Policy Association, World Affairs Center, 345 East 46th Street, New York 17, N.Y.

Books, U.S.A., Inc., P.O. Box 1960, Washington 1, D.C.

Write to the National Education Association Committee on International Relations for free brochure.

For information regarding any field of educational specialization, write to the Executive Secretary of the pertinent NEA Department, Division, Commission or Committee. Regarding foreign travel and tours to the UN write to the Educational Travel Division of the NEA. To obtain a free copy of the NEA Publications Catalog write to Publications Sales Section, NEA.

It is recommended that individual students do not write for materials unless they do it for the whole class.

3530

BAR + POCKET